When God Comes Close

A Journey through Scripture

Rea McDonnell, S.S.N.D.

With a foreword by Carroll Stuhlmueller, C.P.

St. Paul Books & Media

Nihil Obstat: Rev. Thomas W. Buckley, S.T.D.

Imprimatur: +Bernard Cardinal Law

March 11, 1994

Library of Congress Cataloging-in-Publication Data

McDonnell, Rea.
    When God comes close : a journey through Scripture /
Rea McDonnell ; with a foreword by Carroll Stuhlmueller.
        p. cm.
        ISBN 0-8198-8271-2
        1. God—Biblical teaching. 2. Spiritual life—Catholic authors.
I. Title.
BS544.M34   1994
220.6 ' 1—dc20   94-1614
                                                              CIP

The Scripture quotations in this volume were translated by the author.

Portions of this book have appeared in *Prayer Pilgrimage through Scripture*, written by Rea McDonnell, S.S.N.D., published in 1984 by Paulist Press, now out of print.

Cover credit: Sr. Helen Rita Lane, FSP

Printed and published in the U.S.A. by St. Paul Books & Media, 50 St. Paul's Avenue, Boston, MA 02130

St. Paul Books & Media is the publishing house of the Daughters of St. Paul, an international congregation of women religious serving the Church with the communications media.

1 2 3 4 5 6 7 8 9   99 98 97 96 95 94

Contents

Dedication

To Rachel Callahan, C.S.C., Mary Irving S.S.N.D.,
and our mother, Rose.

Foreword

At the beginning of *When God Comes Close*, Sister Rea McDonnell, S.S.N.D., asks us to form a word-image of God. This perception is a key, unlocking the mysteries of our personality as created by God. In what relationship do we see ourselves with God? Do we perceive God as Father or Mother, Lover or Friend, Healer or Teacher, One who forgives or One who comforts, One who crosses boundaries to covenant with outsiders? God is all of these qualities, but God is also one of them especially for each of us.

Sister Rea offers another way to unlock the secret effectiveness of this book. I think of an image which she cites, given to us by one of the disciples of the prophet Isaiah: namely, God as sowing the seed of the word and tenderly nurturing its new growth as it pushes its way out of the earth, attracted by the warmth of sunlight. The passage in Isaiah reads:

> As high as the heavens are above the earth,
> so high are my ways above your ways,
> and my thoughts above your thoughts.
> Just as rain and snow fall from the heavens,
> and do not return till they have soaked the earth,
> making it fertile and fruitful,

yielding seed for sowing,
and bread for eating,
so shall my word be
that issues from my mouth;
it shall not return to me empty,
but shall do what I please,
achieving the purpose for which I sent it.

(Isaiah 55:8-11)

Isaiah recognizes by faith the exalted mystery of God's plans and desires—as high as the heavens are above the earth. Issuing from the mouth of God, the sacred word does not remain suspended in mid-air like rolling, fluffy clouds, myriad in color and in ever changing contours. Rather, God's word soaks the earth and returns to us clothed in earthly vesture. This growth of God's word within us baffles and intrigues us. It is too powerful to ignore, too elusive to understand. It develops within us with loving bondedness and absolute fidelity.

This mystery of God's love and fidelity—*hesed* and *'emet*, according to the Hebrew words which Sister Rea quotes at times from the revelation to Moses on Mount Sinai (Exodus 34:6-7)—reaches beyond our understanding. God loves us more than we will ever realize, even after an eternity in heaven, and will remain forever faithful in that love. In this book Sister Rea does not try the impossible, nor tire us with tedious repetition, to grasp God's love and fidelity. Instead, she invites us into a relationship with God, and there to intuit and glimpse from afar, yet paradoxically from closely within us, what is beyond our comprehension. She also asks us to share this intuition with others while reading and studying God's word in the Bible. Each new person adds another coloration and another form to God's *hesed* and *'emet*, so that the mystery is compounded and reaches new depths and new heights. We remember that impossible prayer in the letter to the Ephesians:

...to know the love of Christ
that surpasses knowledge (3:19).

Paul wants us to know what cannot be known! Our reach must exceed our grasp. Perhaps the axiom should read: to know what can never be known exhaustively. What we come to know through the Scriptures, especially through the guidance of Sister Rea and our adult Bible study companions, contains the exhilarating encouragement: we are certainly on the right track, and with confidence we await an eternity of exploring the mysteries of God's *hesed* and *'emet*.

God's word falls gently like winter snow and spring rain, to soak the earth and so to make the earth fertile and fruitful. This same word soaks our minds and hearts. Just as snow and rain respect the kind of soil they fall upon and respond to the climatic conditions of the area, likewise, God's word exercises immense human respect. Our background and experience, our life vocation, our family and community, our health, physical and emotional, and age of life—all of these personal circumstances become the earth in which God's word settles, to strengthen and console, to illumine and direct.

In this book of Sister Rea's, we come to adult Bible study as real persons in all the raw and magnificent reality of ourselves. Rather than feel hindered or blocked by these circumstances, each facet of our person helps us to appreciate God's *hesed* and *'emet*, love and fidelity. In fact, even our sinfulness reinforces our perception of God's faithfulness, forgiving us "seventy times seven" (Matthew 18:22), or as God said to Moses on Mount Sinai, in the very same passage where God characterizes the divine self as *hesed* and *'emet*: "continuing kindness for a thousand generations, forgiving wickedness and crime and sin" (Exodus 34:7). Such is the fidelity of God.

The prophecy of Isaiah imparts a sturdy confidence: "achieving the purpose for which I sent it," the word. As just mentioned, God does not coerce, nor push and shove, but attracts us by love and fidelity. The relationship between God and ourselves comes from a revelation of God's deepest, personal self, from the word which contains God's hopes and ideals for each of us and for all of us in a communion of faith. This word contacts our deepest self, where we treasure hopes and ideals for ourselves individually, for each member of our family or community. Little wonder that the word is completely and absolutely effective; the word bonds together God and ourselves at our best. Consequently, as Sister Rea points out, we grow out of fear into faith and freedom, out of isolation into the loving bonds of family and community, out of a dying condition into one of new life.

For this to happen, Sister Rea leads us first personally and then as an adult Bible study group through the Gospel of Luke to bond with a compassionate God, through the Gospel of John to recognize God's closeness to ourselves. Each book or sacred writer received God's revelation in the "soil" of his or her unique personality. Here God's word developed and matured, just as God wanted, with the coloration and contour of a St. Luke or a St. John, a Moses or an Isaiah.

I join the many adult Bible study groups around the country, in welcoming this excellent volume. It is, indeed, happy news that St. Paul Books & Media is publishing this book, much enriched from the life experiences of Sister Rea in the years since Paulist Press published her *Prayer Pilgrimage through Scripture* (1984). This edition reflects the teaching and learning, listening to the spiritual journeys of others and contemplating, which Sister Rea has added to her curriculum vitae, since that first book in biblical spirituality.

By persevering in praying with Scripture, and through Bible study under the guidance of this excellent book, each participant in the group will grow and mature spiritually, will bloom beautifully with his or her own unique blend of personality.

God's word close within us will not return to God empty, but will achieve the transforming effect for which God sent it from heaven to earth.

Carroll Sthulmueller, C.P.

Introduction

When God comes close, what an adventure! The human response to divine mystery may, however, be both fascination and fear. Moses, trembling, asked God's name, and felt God's force until finally the face of Moses was radiant with joy.

When God comes close to us, it is not to frighten us but to heal our fear, forgive our failure, and wrap us in an embrace of faithful, steady, unconditional love. God longs to come close, and invites us to deepest intimacy. As I write, I hope and pray that you may find God utterly fascinating, and that gradually you may be a radiant witness of God's tender, faithful love.

Grateful to God for the opportunity to teach biblical spirituality for twenty years, I offer this book to help Christians become more comfortable with Scripture, to make the word of God their home.

"If you make my word your home, you will be my disciples, you will know the truth and the truth will set you free" (John 8:32). To be a disciple, according to its Latin meaning, *discipulus/a*, is to be a learner, a student. Jesus, according to John's Gospel, wants us to be at home in his word so that we can learn from him, be his disciples. Then his truth will set us free. That is God's ultimate design for us all: freedom.

14

God's will is our freedom. To accept this gift of freedom from God, Jesus invites us not only to study and know Scripture, but to become comfortable with the word of God. We are called to be lifelong students, learning from Jesus who is the Word. The truth which his Spirit continually teaches us will continually, day by day, be setting us free. My primary hope for all of us is that we will make Christ's word our home, we will be his disciples, we will learn truth and that truth will set us free.

Another hope is to deepen our knowledge of Jesus Christ and the One who sent him, the One who comes close. This is eternal life, "to know you, the one true God, and the one whom you have sent" (John 17:1-3). Like Paul, all I want for us as we study and pray and share these Scriptures "is to know Christ Jesus and the power of his resurrection" (Philippians 3:10). May this book stir up our desire, our wanting to know Christ Jesus. Scripture itself will stir up the power of Jesus' resurrection, the power we call the Holy Spirit, in the hearts and in the communities of us all.

First I underline the value of our using Scripture to deepen our relationship with God/Jesus/Spirit. Then I move into the Scriptures themselves. After an introduction to each scriptural topic or book, I present the heart of each chapter: a selection of Scripture passages to read, study, pray and share. To guide your praying these Scriptures, I offer brief comments and/or questions on each passage. Finally, in each chapter, I suggest exercises to help embody the biblical understandings and experiences. These are best shared in a family or group of adults.

I am grateful to all who have shaped my praying and living the Scriptures: friends, students, directees, clients, and especially the School Sisters of Notre Dame. I thank God for my nieces, Marie and Angie McDonnell; in loving them so fiercely I have come to know more deeply God's passionate love for us.

Part One

1. The Word of God

If once in our history we had little direct access to the Bible, we are blessed in this century with Popes who have fostered the study of Scripture. In 1943, in his encyclical *Divino Afflante Spiritu*, Pius XII urged Roman Catholic scholars to work with Protestant scripture scholars. We were encouraged to apply critical methods to uncover the texts, the theology, the situations in the life of the biblical authors and their communities from which the Scriptures arose.

Next, Pope John XXIII realized that sometimes our ancient truths were obscured by language which no longer communicated clearly. He called the Second Vatican Council so that our bishops might give a new interpretation which truly would offer *good* news not only to Catholics but to all peoples. Both Pope Paul VI and Pope John Paul II have encouraged not only the study of the good news, but also our sharing its meaning for our own lives in small groups of lay Catholics. In that way we will be better prepared to "give an account of the hope that is in us," as we are urged in the first letter of Peter (1 Peter 3:15). We will be better able to speak with conviction about the God whom we meet when we read, study, pray and share Scripture.

Even with the Church's renewed interest in Scripture, you and I were most likely taught in grade and in high school, not with the Scriptures themselves, but with Bible stories. These stories communicated something of God's power and saving love. Originally, stories told by Jewish and Christian folk were the seeds of our own Jewish Scriptures and New Testament. Because the early Christians knew the stories of their Jewish ancestors, they were able to apply the Jewish Scriptures to their own daily living and to the life of Jesus himself.

Like many peoples, the biblical authors knew that storytelling is an important means of communicating truth. The story tells more than the literal truth. It carries overtones and undercurrents of emotion, of meaning, of action.

Scripture offers us the person, presence, and power of God, not doctrine, not geographical, scientific or even necessarily historical truth. As the Vatican II document on Scripture states: we find in Scripture that truth which is necessary for our salvation. Our salvation-needs change, grow, expand, and this Word nourishes them with the living, loving truth, God's own self, which we need at the time. God comes close to touch our hearts with a deeper truth than mere accuracy.

Stories *do* capture the heart of the listener and introduce the hearer to mystery. Whatever we do in the remainder of this book, let us always approach these Scriptures, these stories of God in relationship with us, with a sense of awe, a sense of mystery.

Mystery is a reality which we will never finish exploring. Catholic theologian Karl Rahner describes mystery as that which is infinitely knowable. Because mystery calls us to keep on wondering, questioning, studying, we will never be finished learning more, digging more deeply, understanding more keenly all that God wants to communicate to us. God especially wants to reveal and communicate all that God is, God's own self, the ultimate Mystery. God wants to come close.

Scripture invites us to an ever deeper relationship with ultimate mystery who is God. Scripture, the living Word of God, has caused a major shift in our spirituality over the past decades. By spirituality I simply mean our relationship with God/Jesus/Spirit. To be in relationship with Mystery means we are forever learning, exploring, listening. We deepen this relationship by asking to hear and understand all God wants to share with us. And we do this relating, learning and deepening in community.

In religion we have gradually moved away from rugged individualism. Instead of stressing an individualized private salvation derived from private prayer, private devotions, private reception of the sacraments, now we pray and worship as a people. Instead of looking to heaven for Jesus or God, we have begun to experience God or Jesus on earth, not only in worship but also in the interaction of the community.

Through that important shift to community in our understanding and practice of spirituality, we were already becoming a biblically formed people. Biblical people are above all community people, those who can recognize God at work not only in their individual lives but also in their community life.

Another important shift in our spirituality has been our experience that God takes the initiative in all spiritual development. It is God who tries to come close to us. In the past we took much initiative. We used self-control and will power, we made sacrifices and we earned merit. We were working our way to heaven, and God would bless us with a final seal of approval once we had done all we should. How, then, have we come to place such great emphasis on God's initiative in our salvation?

Through Scripture study we have come to know these two basic principles: first, we are a people, a community; secondly, God takes the initiative in relating with us, saving us. In Latin America, where the bishops put the Scriptures in the hands of the ordinary folk long ago, many people are experiencing an immense renewal of faith in Christ, experiencing trust in one another as Christ's new community. As we too in North America begin to read, study, talk about, and pray with the Scriptures, we can hope for a rich renewal of the life of the Spirit. Let us look first, then, at the God who takes initiative.

God's Initiative

Our God is one who wants to be known. In the pages of Scripture we are invited to know our God. Through the prophets, through the psalmists, through the stories of encounters with Adam and Abraham, through wrestling with Jacob and arguing with Moses, God tries to communicate all that God is. In the New Testament God continues to reveal through Jesus and the Spirit. Today, through our prayer and through our history, God is eager to communicate. God continually reaches out to lure people like us into mystery. God wants to come close.

God reveals through our prayer. When Abraham begs God to spare Sodom and Gomorrah, when Moses pleads for his people with his arms outstretched, when Hannah weeps so bitterly over her barrenness that her prayer seems like drunken murmuring, the "answer to prayer" is the presence of God, faithful and loving. Our God's face is turned toward those in need, our God's heart is devoted to their/our welfare. "My plans for you are plans of peace, not disaster" (Jeremiah 29:11).

Again and again, God is characterized in the Jewish Scriptures by two Hebrew terms, *hesed* and *'emet*. Various

English translations indicate the rich depths of these words, which are almost untranslatable. *Hesed* means kindness, mercy, tenderness, a love which is abundant, extravagant, unconditional. *'Emet* means faithfulness, consistency, a devotion which lasts forever. The two words are frequently linked. Our translations might read: everlasting love, tender mercy, covenant love, unconditional love, kindness which endures forever, faithful love, unfailing mercy, etc. Through their prayer the biblical people experienced God's steadfast love and devotion, experienced God's *hesed* and *'emet*. In their personal and community prayer, ordinary people met the Mystery who loves them so faithfully.

Through their keen observation of their human history, the Jewish people saw God at work. God reveals through history, the events which shape a particular people. Always and everywhere the Israelites believed that God was active in their history: choosing a people, freeing a people, saving a people, leading a people, scolding a people, punishing a people, forgiving a people, haranguing a people, delighting a people, prospering a people. Whatever the historical event, whatever the geographical movement, whatever the political fortunes or failures, people of faith could see God at work in Israel.

God Forms A People

All that God once did for ancient Israel, God continues to do for us, the new people of God. It took God forty years in the Sinai desert to shape a grumbling, ungrateful group of ex-slaves into a community. God continues to call people together, inviting us to gather a community with whom to share our study of and prayer with Scripture. We do not need to be scholars nor expert at prayer. We just need to be people to form a group, willing to listen together to God, who communicates through the Word and through one another.

We also need some time, a regular time, preferably once a week for six to eight weeks. October-November and February-March have proved to be relatively uncrowded months. In the beginning a group of four might take only thirty minutes; a group of eight might need an hour. It is helpful to keep a strict starting and ending time and not to exceed two hours.

Our Scripture group might include friends, neighbors, parishioners, perhaps even some adult relatives. The only qualification is their willingness to read and pray with Scripture and to risk speaking personally in the group about what happened when they prayed. They may share God's message, God's prodding, God's presence or absence, God's work in their personal daily life. A group of mixed ages and genders can be ideal. Homogenous groups, such as college students or housewives or senior citizens or vowed religious or business executives or cursillistas or that Renew group which shared so well three years ago, are also effective.

God may want to form a small community through Scripture, prayer and you. Don't decide now. Let this be a seed. Further possibilities and instructions, set off in the text, will thread through this book.

Scripture as Sacrament

If God reveals God's own self through the pages of Scripture, through the stories of the Jewish people, through the history of the Judeo-Christian community, then we who read and digest and incorporate this revealing word are deeply encountering our God who wants so much to be known. We might even say that because of this encounter, Scripture itself is a sacrament. If sacraments are outward signs designed to "give grace," then reading, praying, sharing Scripture is a sacrament. The Bible is certainly an outward sign, something we can hear and see and read and touch and sing. Does Scripture "give grace?" What is grace but the life of God? In Scripture we have an external sign of God's communicating God's very life, presence and activity. Scripture brings us to communion with God. It leads us into grace-life through our reading, our studying, our praying, our sharing Scripture. This is life in abundance: to know our God and Jesus, the one sent.

Sacraments do what they signify. The bread of heaven feeds us, the anointing with oil heals us. This word of God, Scripture, does what it signifies: "The word that goes forth from my mouth does not return to me empty but carries out my will and succeeds in doing that for which it was sent" (Isaiah 55:11).

Scripture does what it says. For example, when we read in the New Testament about Jesus healing the man born blind (John 9), the risen Lord here and now is giving us light. He is here and now healing blindness in us. As we read those words of healing and become involved with the word, we are participating in the risen Christ's light-giving activity right now. Whether we are sitting quietly in the back of church, working in the yard, or driving the car, Jesus is always in the process of giving us light. This encounter is union with our light-giving Lord. This encounter is possible because we are in contact with the word of God, which does what it symbolizes.

Scripture brings God's/Jesus'/Spirit's action into our current time and place. If we are reading about the multiplication of the loaves 2,000 years ago, that story nourishes us now. If we are reading the story of the foot washing, Jesus' action for his disciples is his foot washing action right now for us. If we read the story of the paralytic let down through the roof, we are at this moment being brought (in whatever our spiritual or emotional paralysis) to Jesus for new freedom, new movement.

To read Scripture, then, is to know God, to encounter Christ, to let the Spirit act in our history. Scripture is an outward sign which brings us into union with God, Christ and Spirit, and thus "gives grace."

Jesus is the primary sacrament, the one through whom we meet God most intimately. The early Christians, of course, saw and heard and touched with their hands this word of God, Jesus (1 John 1:1). They experienced Jesus in the flesh. They experienced not only his life but his dying and rising. It is that dying and rising of Jesus which is the very core of the New Testament.

After their experience, the disciples reflected on that experience and then moved into action. They proclaimed the good news, they carried on the mission and ministry of Jesus, they articulated the stories of his life and their life. These stories eventually became our Scriptures, the New Testament. We will look at the first disciples' experience, their reflection, and their action in the second part of this book. As we ponder their reflection on their experience of Christ, we hope that our own reflection may lead us to an ever deepening experience of God/Jesus/Spirit come close.

Praying Scripture

"This is eternal life: to know you, the one true God." When John the Evangelist first proclaimed that sentence he had two audiences: Greek and Jewish. For the Greeks the word "know" means to contemplate. For them contemplation means standing back and peering through their eyelashes in order to penetrate the deep underlying realities. For the Jews, to "know" signifies union, intimate contact, experience. It is through Jesus, the word of God, that we can contemplate, experience, know God. "You will know that I am in my Father, you are in me, and I am in you." When we hear this word, read this word, know this word, our knowledge that God is in us and we are in God has passed from knowledge of our union into actual union. The word of God does what it says.

Union with God is the hope of all our prayer. To contemplate Scripture is to experience God. To savor a word of Scripture is to pray, a way of tasting and seeing how good God is.

There are days when we can read a few lines of Scripture and move to affective prayer, our hearts on fire with love for God. Sometimes Scripture gives us spirit for effective ministry. Sometimes we rest, at home in God's word, in a kind of silent union.

There are other days when the pavement has been hard, the bus ride interminable, the students difficult, the patients quarrelsome, the baby screaming with colic. Spontaneous praise or petition just cannot arise through the headache, the bleary eyes, the aching back, the short temper. A passage of Scripture leads only to sleep, or to that kind of nothingness which evokes a nagging guilt that one is really not praying at all. At such times, when we open Scripture, God sends a powerful word to us, a word which will not return empty but which will do what it says. This word, even if we are too exhausted to feel it, will nourish us, cleanse us, free us, heal us, light up our dark places, plunge us into union with God.

To spend a time of prayer simply reading Scripture is, in itself, prayer. St. Teresa of Avila teaches that prayer is conversation with the One whom we know loves us. The Word of God is God's part of the conversation. It is the word of God which takes the initiative, which accomplishes this prayer and praise. God's word returns fruitful, having done that for which it was sent, having united us with God.

2. Images of God

At the core of Israel's religion is the First Commandment of the Decalogue: "I am the Lord your God. You
shall not have strange gods before me." To protect themselves from all types of idols, from golden calf to decora-
tive murals, they were forbidden to make any images of
God. Yet to communicate their experience of God, the
Israelite authors of Scripture sought verbal images to
express their understanding of God and how God acted
on behalf of the people. They imaged God as shepherd,
king, rock, dew, warrior, husband, companion, and
more.

At first, in their more primitive religious experience,
the Israelites knew their God to be God of all the gods,
king of the heavenly court of many gods, obviously highest of all gods because theirs was a God who does justice
(Psalm 82). Gradually they came to understand that there
is only one God, a God full of compassion, faithful and
kind (Exodus 34:6). Strange gods, idols, still lurk, however, whenever we try to pin God down, hem God in,
define God.

God Is More Than We Can Say

Biblical writers, expressing the faith of the people,
knew God as personal, even called God a person. They

searched their human experience and saw human beings as the crown of creation (Psalm 8). Therefore God must be a person, the highest compliment they could pay. Yet we know that all language about God is analogy. God is not a person. God is more than a person.

There is no language which can express who God is in "himself." Thus, for me just to have written "himself" is only a minuscule part of the truth of who God really is. God is neither masculine nor feminine. There can be no definition of God, because to define means, literally from its Latin root, to set limits. The mystery of who God is goes far beyond our language.

The people of Israel wanted to know God's name. God tells Moses, at the beginning of their relationship, that God is YHWH, Yahweh, the one who is. Moses asks for more, many chapters later in the book of Exodus (Exodus 33, 34). Show me your glory, he begs God. I will show you my beauty, God promises. Setting Moses in a cleft of a rock, God passes by, crying out a new name:

The Lord, the Lord, a God compassionate and gracious, slow to anger and rich in kindness (*hesed*) and faithfulness (*'emet*).

Various images, ever new names, preserve us from a rigidity of thought which would try to limit God. No one name or image can exhaust the mystery of God, the one who is infinitely knowable.

Through the variety of the biblical authors' experiences of God, we are able to resonate with the God of our own experience. God was and is present in their and our ordinary events of life: love and work, problems, peace, and pain.

"In many and various ways God spoke of old to our ancestors..." (Hebrews 1:1). To describe those many and various ways, the authors used verbal images of God throughout the books of Scripture. They were aware of the limits which language imposed on them. God is a rock (Psalm 40), but how much more than a rock. God is dew (Hosea 14:5), but how much more than dew.

Perhaps before Jesus, the deepest way in which the Hebrew people experienced their God was not in thunder and fire or even gentle breezes (1 Kings 19:11-14). They knew God in their most intimate moments of human love.

Our first human love is directed to our parents. Thus, we find that God is called Father (for example, in Jeremiah 3:4) but also imaged as mother (for example, in Isaiah 49:14-15 and 66:13).

For adults, love turns to courtship with all its joy of being wanted and chosen, with exquisite emotions of tenderness, despair at separation, longing, ecstasy. The biblical book, Song of Songs, captures in allegory that type of love between God and God's beloved Israel. Our adult love, however, so vulnerable and trusting, can be betrayed. Through the experience of the prophet Hosea's broken marriage (Hosea 1, 3), God tries to communicate how painful is Israel's scorning of God's faithful love (*hesed* and *'emet*). Human love is often the model, the instrument, the sacrament of God's tender fidelity.

Notice that characteristic of our God is a loving, faithful relationship. God is always described in the Scriptures as "for us." Rather than offering philosophical definitions of supreme being, uncaused cause, omnipotent and omniscient, our biblical authors describe God not so much as a being but as a doer. God acts, and acts always on our behalf.

Even the images of God imply action. God's "rockness" is steady for us to cling to, God's "dewiness" is gentle to cause our growth, God's shepherding is toward pastures to nourish us with abundance, God's warring is to protect us from enemies on every side.

Unless we are literalists or fundamentalists, we know that God's portrayal as warrior or father is not the whole truth. Our human experience of God cries out for words to express God. The best we can say is that God is like a person, like a warrior on the side of justice, like a father to Jesus and to us. To the Israelites, to Jesus, and to some of us, God is also like a mother. God is greater than, more than, either parent or both parents together.

God is more than father, mother, everyone and everything. We call God parent or warrior or gentle dew or steady rock only by analogy. God is more than we can say, and we may not have false gods, absolutized images, in place of God's mystery.

Images of God as warrior, or descriptions of God as furious cause many of us to cringe. How can God sanction war, let alone lead people to battle?

We must remember that in Scripture we have stories of people's faith experience, not definitions of God's person and nature. Since the Israelites needed to fight defensively and sometimes wanted to fight offensively, since their entire life was permeated by their relationship with God, it was natural for them to find God in their camps, their citadels. They "put not (their) trust in horses," in battle (Psalm 33), but only in God, whom they believed they honored by their battles. After all, popes led crusades in what we like to call more civilized times. Priests and Catholic people in this country celebrated Masses of thanksgiving when the United States bombed Japan not many years ago. As our own faith experience develops, over centuries and even decades, we gradually come to know, as a people, that our God is a God of peace.

God and Anger

What of God's anger, sometimes depicted in the Jewish Scriptures as relentless fury? If we believe God is imaged best as a real person in a real relationship with us, then we must admit that in real relationships anger will always have a relatively important role. It may be that we have had terrifying experiences of another's anger directed at us. The deeper the relationship with that person, the deeper the terror, it seems.

Because our Christian spirituality emphasizes the image of God as father (or even mother) and because most of us were terrified by our parents' anger with us (see *Denial of Death*, by Ernst Becker) we can project that kind of anger onto God. We may expect that kind of anger from God. In reading of God's anger, we might experience again that kind of fear which stems from our profound helplessness as our parent towers over us. Even the best, the kindest of parents "towers" over the naughty child.

It is helpful for us, as "Christians come of age" (Dietrich Bonhoeffer), as Christians in adult relationships, to remember our most loving, deep adult relationship. How is anger expressed in that relationship? How do you prefer to have this dearest person's anger expressed to you? What happens after the storm is spent? What does the relationship look like a week later?

For Jews and for Christians alike, it is important to express all our emotions in prayer. If God seems angry with us, we often feel angry with what we perceive as God's interference in our life and plans. Anger in a real and healthy relationship cannot be expressed only by one party. Our reading about God's anger in Scripture can awaken us to our own anger in our relationship with God.

As with a faithful, loving friend or spouse, we can hear God's anger, receive it, repent, cooperate as God transforms us. God's anger will not destroy us.

And so, in a real relationship with a real God, we can express our anger to God in prayer. God cannot be destroyed by our rage (see *May I Hate God?*, by Pierre Wolff, S.J., Paulist Press). God too repents (Amos 7:1-6). If once

God chastised us, now God heals (Hosea 6:1); if once God abandoned us in fury, now God names us beloved forever (Isaiah 54:6-10).

In healthy human relationships anger expresses intimacy and trust. Anger is neither right nor wrong. Anger is God's gift to us, a power, hopefully a motivator toward more justice in the world. Healthy anger is a signal that justice has been thwarted, that boundaries have been violated, that evil is prevailing, that we are in danger. The feeling of anger is a signal and gives us energy for action.

Anger need not always be acted on, however. It need not be violent in act or word, need not oppress or violate others in return. Instead of doing violence to ourselves when we feel anger, instead of judging anger and stomping it down, if we get curious about its origins we become more aware of ourselves and our motives and gradually we become more free, learning little by little how to express our anger appropriately.

Anger, even anger with God, is best communicated. Sometimes in gentle, sometimes in forceful ways, but always in fair ways, anger is best felt, thought about, decided on and finally communicated directly. If it is denied, shoved underground, and covered over, anger will eventually manifest itself in skewed ways, harmful to oneself or to relationships. Healthy anger does not blame, does not explode, does not punish, does not stem from a sense of entitlement, but is communicated simply, respectfully, and then let go. (For further understanding of this important passion in our lives—and in our life with God—see *Words Made Flesh*, by Sister Fran Ferder, Ave Maria Press, 1986.)

New Testament Images

In the New Testament, Jesus offers us other intimate images of God. His unique contribution to our understanding of God may be his calling God "Abba." The

Jewish people knew God to be Father, but the intimate "Abba" is Jesus' expression of total trust and vulnerability in relationship. In Mark's portrayal of the agony in the garden, Jesus, tortured by fear, cries "Abba," "my Father!" Paul uses the name twice as he teaches us that the Spirit of the risen Jesus is deep in our innermost being, crying "Abba" (Galatians 4:6, Romans 8:15). It seems that a privileged expression of our relationship with God is "Abba"—a word which we cannot appropriate to ourselves but which is completely dependent on the Spirit's gift, the Spirit's prayer within us.

Two other images of God which Jesus offers us express God's *hesed*, God's passionate devotion to us. Jesus calls God a shepherd, an image well known to the psalmists (Psalms 23 and 80) and to the prophets (Ezekiel 34). What may be special to Jesus' own century, however, is the disdain of the people for shepherds. According to Joachim Jeremias in *Jerusalem in the Time of Jesus*, all shepherds were considered guilty of thieving by reason of their profession. In Luke 15:1-10, then, when Jesus likens his Father to a good shepherd, he underscores his Father's devotion to the sinner, the maligned, the outcast. God, as shepherd, does not hesitate even to be identified with the unclean. Luke adds an intimate touch to the story found in Matthew 18:12-14: the shepherd in Luke lifts the lost sheep to his shoulder and carries it.

Immediately following the image of God as shepherd, Luke's Gospel offers another image showing God aligned with the most outcast group in the Jewish community: women. "If a woman has ten silver pieces and loses one of them...." God searching for lost people is like a woman searching for her coin. God is like an ordinary housewife.

Jesus, Image of God

Whether we search the Jewish Scriptures or the New Testament, we discover images of God expressive of human longing to see the face of God, to hear God's voice to savor God's taste. All these human expressions fall short. But, as in any relationship, the lover wants to reveal himself or herself to the beloved. So we are not dependent on merely human striving to know God, on human searches to understand the Lord.

Once again God takes the initiative and reveals God's own self in the perfect image, communicates God's most inner life in a perfect expression of just who God is—for us. We call that perfect image "Jesus."

As the author of Hebrews phrases it, Jesus is "the express image of God's person" (1:3). Paul directly calls Jesus the image of God, but John the evangelist portrays the entire human history of the Word as Jesus' imaging his Father. Jesus acts and works only as he sees the Father acting and working. He speaks only what he hears the Father speaking. "If anyone sees me, Philip, that person sees the Father" (John 14:9).

All verbal images, all human words, fall silent in the presence of the Word of God, Jesus. Jesus completely expresses what and who God is. He expresses God's loves and hates, God's desires and angers.

God is expressed in the humanness of Jesus, not "good old plastic Jesus" of the car's dashboard. Jesus is not God in thin disguise but a real *human* being, who bleeds, cries, sweats, rages, sleeps, sings, and enjoys banquets. That is the scandal, and the glory of the incarnation.

Our God wanted to be immersed in flesh, *sarx*, the Greek word for butcher meat. The Word became *sarx*. As *sarx*, Jesus grew in wisdom and age and grace, becoming ever more human, ever more expressing God's life within him.

He grew in wisdom, learning from life, relationships, community, God. He grew in grace, ever opening
to receive more and more of God's own life. As he grew
more human, he thus grew more divine, more and more
full of God. He who emptied himself (Philippians 2) was
being filled day by day with God, with *hesed* and *'emet*.
Jesus put a body on God's faithful love. To see Jesus'
compassionate devotion in action was to see God's compassion in the flesh.

Jesus worked through all the developmental stages
we work through. He had both his cranky days, and the
days when he flowed in total "sync" with life. He was
affected by seasons and sunshine, moods and mysteries
until he became so fully human that he pioneered the
promise to humanity: we all are made in the image of God.

In Jesus our human potential gradually became reality. "Oh wondrous exchange," our liturgy sings, for we
are, in Christ, becoming divinized. We too grow in wisdom and grace. We too image God to our broken world.

Guided Prayer

(I suggest that each day you concentrate on only one
of the following passages, so that during the day your
mind and heart might return to the God revealed in that
passage. The guiding material may not help you pray. I
suggest you read the Scripture passage without looking
at the guiding comments and follow your own intuitions,
feelings, and movements of the heart. When the passage
"dries up" for you, try the guiding material.)

Psalm 68:1-10, 19-20

God arises. God's enemies are scattered and
those who hate God flee. The just rejoice and exult

before God; they are glad and sing praise. Sing to God, chant praise to God's name, applaud God who rides on the clouds. Our God is the father of orphans and the defender of widows—such is God in the holy dwelling.

God gives a home to the forsaken and leads prisoners out into freedom. O God, when you went forward, leading your people, when you marched through the wilderness, the earth quaked. Rain fell from heaven in the presence of our God, the Holy One.

You showered a generous rain upon us, O God. You restored the worn out land. Your people settled there, and in your goodness, you provided for the needy.

Day by day, our God is blessed, our God who bears our burdens. Our God is a God who saves.

God is imaged as warrior, father, defender, leader, provider, burden-bearer and savior. God bears our burdens day after day. Unlike the capricious, demanding gods of the ancient middle east, our god is a God who saves. And God does not work only on behalf of ancient peoples. What God once did, God continues to do for us. God frees us, dignifies us, protects us—not always in ways which we can recognize, but God does save. We are often lonely and feel imprisoned; we are a worn out land, often poor and needy.

Give your burdens to God right now. Show God where in your life you feel oppressed, helpless, injured, poor. Let God bear these burdens, these feelings, for you and with you. Pray the psalm again. Change the word "God" to "you," and address God personally.

Hosea 2:21-22

> I will espouse you to myself forever, says our
> God. I will hold you to myself in holiness and
> justice. I will take hold of you with my mercy and
> my kindness. I will espouse you with faithfulness
> and you shall know me.

In the opening chapters of the book of Hosea the prophet, God is imaged as a husband and a lover. Tell God directly how you want to be loved. Where in your life do you need God to do justice, where do you need God's kindness? How does it feel for God to take hold of you? Scary? Secure? Peaceful? Share these feelings with God, who accepts you just the way you are. You do not have to earn God's love. The holiness in which God wraps you is *God's* holiness, not yours. Try to rest and let God love you. Read Isaiah 35. We select some verses which image God as a gardener and as a healer.

> Deserts and parched lands blossom, blooming
> with flowers in abundance. Streams burst open in
> the desert, pools of water among the burning sands.
> The eyes of the blind will be opened, and the ears of
> the deaf unstopped. The lame will leap like deer
> and the tongues of the dumb will sing.

When has God strengthened you, steadied you, opened your eyes and ears, changed your dry places into a lush garden? Ask the Spirit to help you remember, and be as concrete as possible in your memories. How do these memories make you feel? Share those feelings with your gardening God.

Psalm 146

> Praise our God! Praise God, O my heart! I will
> praise God for as long as I live. I want to sing to my
> God all my life.

Do not put trust in human leaders, for how can they save you?

When they die they return to the earth and all their plans perish.

Happy are we who have the God of Jacob and Rachel to save us.

Happy are we who can depend on our God, who created the heaven, earth, seas and everything that lives.

God always keeps promises, judges in favor of the oppressed and outcast, and gives food to the hungry.

Our God sets prisoners free, gives sight to the blind, raises all who are humbled and loves those who are set right.

God protects the foreigners in our land, the immigrants, widows and orphans; God ruins the plans of the wicked.

Our God will reign forever!

Israelites did not define God as a being who was/is supreme, all knowing, etc., as the Greeks did. The biblical people rather related to God as a doer, and primarily as a worker of justice for the poor, one who sets people free and cares faithfully for their needs. Notice how God acts in this psalm, how the people experience God at work on their behalf. Again, change the word "God" to "you." Address God personally and directly. Ask the Spirit to remind you just where and when in your lifetime God has done these kinds of things for you. As you remember, try to be very specific in your memories.

Job 38:1-12

Out of the storm God spoke to Job: "How can you speak so ignorantly and cloud my desires?

Stand up and act adult. I will question, and you give me the answers, Job....

"Where were you when I fashioned the earth? Where were you when the cornerstone was laid, when the morning stars sang in chorus and all the children of God shouted for joy?...

Where were you when I shut up the sea as it burst forth from the womb, when I made the clouds its clothing, thick darkness to swaddle the sea?... Have you ever in your lifetime commanded the morning, or shown the sun how to rise?"

Join Job as he stands in awe before the mystery of God. We are so small and insignificant, and we pray to know in our bones that God is *our* higher power, our universe's deepest energy. Little as we are, what is it about our humanness which God loves so much? How can all this creative majesty want to become so united with us that God takes flesh and learns to sing and shout for joy? As you ponder this mystery in your heart, share your feelings, all your feelings, with this awesome God who loves you and wants to come close.

Genesis 32:3-13; 33:1-16

Jacob (who had cheated his brother Esau out of his birthright, his father's blessing, his inheritance and then fled for fear of Esau's fury) sent messengers ahead to Esau with this word: "My lord, your servant Jacob says, I have been living with Laban in a far country. I have oxen, asses and sheep, and I have sent gifts ahead so that I may win your favor." When the messengers returned to Jacob they told him: "We have met your brother on his way here with four hundred men." Very much afraid and distressed, Jacob divided the people and the animals with him into two groups, so that if one were destroyed by Esau the other would survive.

Then Jacob began to pray: "O God of my ancestors, O Lord at whose command I am coming back now to my own country and to my family, you promised me prosperity. I your servant am in no way worthy of all your faithful and loving devotion (*hesed*, *'emet*). When I crossed the Jordan, running away, I had nothing but the staff in my hand, and now I have two companies. Save me, I pray, from my brother Esau, for he will destroy us."

Then Jacob chose the finest of his animals to send as a gift to Esau...Jacob saw Esau coming toward him with his 400 men, so he divided his children between his wives, Leah and Rachel, putting Rachel and Joseph last. Jacob went on ahead, and bowed seven times to the ground as he approached Esau. His brother ran to meet him and embraced him, threw his arms around him and kissed him. They both wept....

Esau asked, "What were all those animals you sent ahead?"

"They were meant to win your favor, my lord."

Esau replied, "I have more than enough.... Let us set out, and I will go at your pace." Jacob answered, "Why should my lord be so kind to me?"

How is God imaged here? Which parable of Jesus does this remind you of? By our standards should not Esau, the betrayed, at least rage at Jacob for a while? They embrace and cry. If human beings can be so forgiving, how much more God!

Perhaps Jesus read and studied and prayed with this story often throughout his life. When he began to tell his own stories about God, the parables, his image of the prodigal son's return is quite like this event.

Speak with God about the relationships in which you have failed, about which you are afraid. Perhaps even your relationship with God. Then remember, and remind God, of those people in your own life who have been kind to you, who have "gone at your pace," and so deepened your capacity for relationship. God accepts us and our pace, and we need send no gifts ahead to win God's favor. We have God's steady and faithful love. Share your feelings and desires now with God.

Genesis 32:24-31

> As Jacob journeyed back, he sent the company across the gorge and he was left alone. A man wrestled with him there until dawn. When the man saw that he could not throw Jacob, he struck him on his hip as they wrestled. The man said, "Let me go, for it is almost morning." Jacob replied, "I will not let you go until you bless me." The man asked Jacob's name, then said: "Your name will no longer be Jacob but Ish-ra-el, because you wrestled with God and with men and you have prevailed."
>
> Jacob said, "Tell me your name." The man replied, "Why do you ask my name?" and he gave Israel his blessing there. Jacob called the place Penu-el because, he said, "I have seen God face to face and yet I live." The sun was rising as Jacob passed through Penuel, limping because of his hip.

We keep asking God's name, asking for new and ever more true images of God; that is our blessing. God here is imaged as a wrestler, for the biblical writers were quick to recognize God. An intimate relationship with God may entail wrestling with God and/or receiving a new name. What name does God give you? Sit quietly and rest your mind, clearing it, quieting it and see what "bubbles up" from the depths of you.

If you receive a name from God, you may spend your time of prayer savoring that name, arguing about that name. No matter what they are, share your feelings about that name with God.

If you draw a blank in this kind of quiet prayer of listening, then try another kind of biblical prayer: remembering. Remember and discuss with God the times in your life when the two of you have wrestled. Show God your wounds—in all your relationships. Show God in great detail how you are still hurting, still limping, and ask for healing.

Exodus 34:6

> "The Lord, the Lord, a God compassionate and gracious, slow to anger, abounding in kindness and fidelity."

The Hebrew word for compassion, *rachum*, is a play on words. The Hebrew word for womb, for uterus, is *rechem*. God's compassion is womb-compassion. "Can a woman forget her baby, a mother forget the child of her womb?" God asks through the prophet Isaiah (49:15): "Even if these forget, I will never forget you, I will not leave you orphaned," promises our God.

Fear of abandonment is a fairly universal terror. Let God speak directly to your heart, to your terror. No matter what we do, God will not leave us. God's compassion, ability to suffer with us, to feel with us, is like a mother's—and so much more. Share with God whatever feelings arise in you.

Genesis 3:21

> Before God cast Adam and Eve out of the garden, God made tunics of skins for them and clothed them.

In our culture, women are usually the ones who sew. God is imaged here as a seamstress , caring for the very ones who have tried to usurp God's place. How do you feel about the image of God as feminine? How do you feel about God's painstaking work envisioned here? Remember how in ancient times, needles were clumsy bits of bone and threads were usually strips of well-chewed animal hide. What do you learn about God from this image? Share your feelings with God.

Two images, or titles, God and Jesus share: good shepherd and savior:

Ezekiel 34:15-16

> "I myself will pasture my sheep, giving them rest," says the Lord God. "Those who are lost I will search out. Those who have strayed I will bring back. Those who are injured I will bandage. The ones who are sick I will heal. The strong and the healthy I will _____ and I will shepherd them rightly."

John 10:14

> "I am the good shepherd. I know my sheep...they recognize my voice."

Notice in the passage from Ezekiel how God designs a unique response to each of our special needs. What do you need/want from God today? Share those desires.

Notice the blank space. In the original Hebrew text the word is missing. What will God do for the strong and healthy?

Our different English translations indicate the spirituality of the different translators. *The New American Bible* claims that God will destroy the strong and healthy; *The*

Revised Standard Version notes that God will watch over them. Translators of *The New English Bible* insert the words: "The strong and the healthy I will set out to play."

How can we know what to put in that missing text? We can look to Jesus, the best image of God. What will Jesus do with the strong and healthy? What do you remember from the Gospels?

In John 10:10 Jesus proclaims: "I have come that you may have life, life in abundance." How could a person so eager to give life want to destroy? He came to make us strong and healthy. When we receive his life in abundance, of course he will set us out to play. Speak with him about your fears and desires regarding intimacy with God.

Psalm 68:20

> Our God is a God who saves.

John 4:42

> Truly this is the savior of the world.

Jesus' name—*Jeshua*—means saving. *Yesh* in Hebrew means to give space, to give room, to set free in the open. Israel's experience of God's saving power, freeing them from slavery in Egypt, was also an experience of much room (the whole Sinai peninsula), and of much time (40 years), to become a people covenanted with God.

Sometimes their freedom frightened them and they longed to return to the security of their slavery. God's saving, or setting free, includes God's presence in the midst of wandering, confusion, and insecurity. Jesus is God-with-us always. Ask to believe this, to trust God's freeing power and presence.

How To Share Faith

Obviously the above passages can be used by oneself. A more fruitful way to use them is to gather in a weekly group meeting for faith sharing. Faith sharing presupposes that you are trying to pray with Scripture regularly. You would meet to share with others how "the word has found a home" in you, how God is working in your own story as you dialogue with God's own story.

In faith sharing I suggest a discipline at which my students have often balked but which eventually "works" to the group's advantage. I suggest that as a person speaks about a Scripture passage and how he or she is challenged or comforted—what memories, desires, feelings it stirred—no one say a word in response.

We are tempted to compare the speaker's journey to our own, we are anxious to assure the timid that we understand, we are quick to make judgments about the speaker's content. Judgments must be set aside—judgments about truth and falsehood, because a person's experience with God is true, uniquely true to him or her; judgments about maturity and immaturity, because a person's human and spiritual development is his or her unique pilgrimage to God; judgments about the beauty, the depth, the giftedness of the faith experience, because we may make insidious comparisons with our own experience's beauty and depth (usually falling far short of the other's) and because the group's members may be tempted to play the game of impressing one another.

After a few meetings my students recognize the advantages of the discipline of not responding verbally. First, no judgments can be expressed and so the private judgments eventually grow less persistent. My students experience themselves as open to receive whatever the speaker will share. Some find God quite present in their own receptivity because they are mirroring God's own receptivity to the speaker.

Secondly, they realize that they are contemplating. Very simply, contemplation means noticing with such total absorption that one's self is forgotten. Music, oceans, sunsets, a baby's fingers can "catch" us in contemplation. Not preparing a verbal response, my students find that they are completely absorbed both in the other person and in God's love and action as revealed by God in the other's story of faith. They realize that as their listening skills are sharpened, their communication skills are broadened. Accustomed to verbalizing, they discover that eyes, smiles, faces, and postures communicate effectively. The medium of faith sharing, the process itself, becomes a message of openness, contemplation, listening to the word and responding with one's body.

Some will prefer a global sharing on all the scripture passages; others may share on just one passage which touched them. Depending on the amount of time available and number of members, a maximum time per person might be agreed on. For example, a 90 minute meeting might allow five people a maximum of 15 minutes each.

I would suggest that after each person has had a chance to share, the meeting end with some quiet absorption time together. The group might decide to hold hands during the silent time. Someone might create a prayer to conclude with, or the Our Father or a hymn might end the meeting.

If at first a group of six meets only for thirty minutes, be patient. As group members grow in trust the meetings may lengthen.

When the group is formed, it might be wise to agree on some ground rules about regular attendance, confidentiality, a maximum time limit, monopolizing, etc. At every second or third meeting, a rotating chairperson could call for a fifteen minute evaluation of the group's process according to the original ground rules.

"Where two or three are gathered together" in Jesus' name, Jesus comes close, revealing God's faithful love for us. We too are instruments of God's respect and care for each of us as we move together on our journey through the Scriptures.

How to Establish a Faith Sharing Group

WHO   You. Invite a group of three to seven people who are willing during each week to pray with Scripture to meet

WHEN   At a specific time for six to eight weeks.

WHERE   In your own or another's home.

WHY   In sharing how God reveals God's presence, love, faithfulness, grace, challenges, comfort, etc., a community will be bonded by the Spirit, each member will be enriched, and God will be praised.

HOW   Before the first meeting, each member should purchase this book. One chapter a week should be assigned, with members using the Scripture in that chapter for prayer. At the first meeting, in a quiet atmosphere, perhaps with a candle and an open Bible as a centerpiece, you will call for introductions and set ground rules for the group.

Ground rules will include:

1. Confidentiality—all names and identities are to be safeguarded;
2. Regular attendance—with a phone call to the leader if someone will be absent;
3. Outside limit of time—longer than two hours usually creates fatigue;

4. Attention to the length of one's own sharing, with an agreement that the leader may interrupt if need be;
5. Agreement to make no verbal comment after each member's sharing;
6. Agreement that any one may simply pass by saying, "I pass," but that passing is not to become a habit.

FORMAT   This will include a simple opening prayer or song or quiet music, some silence after each member's faith sharing, and, at the end, some silent time to absorb. The leader Sassigns the next chapter. A final ritual concludes the meeting: a brief shared prayer or intercessions, an Our Father or hymn, perhaps a kiss of peace.

FOLLOW-UP   In six weeks only about half the chap ters may be used; another six or eight week session could focus on the New Testament chapters.

Exercises

Let your imagination run free. In how many and in what various ways can you describe God-for-you? For example, could God be a bed, cool water on a hot day, a warm fire during winter's storms?

High school teachers often challenge youngsters to rewrite the psalms. Paraphrasing Psalm 23, one teen on probation wrote: "The Lord is my case worker. No reason to run scared." For your own benefit, rewrite your favorite psalm.

Try to dance your image of God. Draw God. Write a haiku poem of three lines, using two syllables, five syllables, two syllables per line to describe God.

What image of you does God prefer? Try to "get inside God's skin" and look at yourself. Are you, for God, a shepherd, a rock, thunder, dew? What name does God call you?

Can you find a group with whom to share your images, your rewritten psalm, your dance, your drawing? You may want to include these exercises in your faith-sharing meeting, after everyone has had a chance to share about their praying with Scripture. That may lengthen the meeting disproportionately, so you may want to find a group different from your faith-sharing group. It may be your family. After a group has worked through the exercises in this book, each member could form his or her own group and walk through this scriptural journey again. One of the beauties of this living word is that a month or a year later, we can come to the Word fresh. This living Word will speak to us in new situations, new relationships.

3. The Leaders

If spirituality is about our relationship with God, in a biblical spirituality we focus on God who initiates the relationship. Our response to God's initiating love may be prayer, but it also may be a response of action.

Much of the Jewish Scripture is devoted to its leaders and how they related with God. God's initiative in these relationships usually took the form of a call to action, a vocation to leadership or prophecy. Like ourselves, these men and women had to trust that their call was not a delusion. They had to risk, usually beginning a pilgrimage through uncharted lands.

In this chapter we will focus on some called to leadership in Israel: Abraham, Joseph, Moses, Joshua, Gideon, Samuel, David and Solomon. You will notice that these leaders, remembered in writing in a patriarchal society, are male. Males were the focus of these accounts, but some women's heroism slips into Israel's history. For example, Moses' mother and sister cleverly save him from death as an infant. Miriam leads liturgy; Rahab signals for Joshua's army; Deborah judges wisely; Jael kills the enemy; Hannah is a model of prayer and Ruth of faithfulness; Isaiah's wife is also a prophet; Judith and Esther are saviors of their people. The mother of seven men tortured by King Antiochus encouraged her sons to faithfulness to God as she watched their mutilation; "this mother was most remarkable of all, and deserves to be remembered with special honor" (2 Maccabees 7:20).

Describing male leaders in chronological order, I will thus be offering an overview of Israel's history. My purpose, like that of the authors of these stories, is not to present historical material, however, but to show God's unfailing care for this people. The response of these leaders models for us various spiritualities, differing ways of relating with God. Finally I will note some overarching themes in the stories of these leaders: how God chooses the weak, makes and renews the covenant, deals with sin, works for human liberation, and expresses law.

Sketches of Israel's Leaders

Abraham is called patriarch, father of the chosen people. He is introduced abruptly in Genesis 12, under command by the Lord to leave his country and family in order to explore new land. God promises a blessing, and promises that Abraham's name itself shall be a blessing. For the Hebrew, blessing means to share in the life of the one who blesses. Thus Abraham is above all called to share God's life. God's life is fruitful, so Abraham's fruitful line begins with the birth of Isaac (Genesis 21) to the matriarch of the community, Sarah.

Isaac's grandson, Joseph, interpreted dreams; he had a kind of call to be God's spokesperson (Genesis 40-41). As redeemer of his family from famine, Joseph became the hero of Israel. More remarkably, he is remembered for forgiving his brothers, the very ones who earlier had sold him into slavery in Egypt. He became a royal official in Egypt, dispensing food during a famine. Coming to Egypt in search of food, but not recognizing Joseph, his brothers pleaded with him. Joseph could no longer control his feelings...Joseph made himself known to his brothers, and "so loudly did he weep" that his attendants heard him. Joseph repeated to his brothers that God had sent him ahead to Egypt to save lives from famine. Then "he kissed all his brothers and wept over them" (Genesis 45).

After remaining in Egypt for some four hundred years, the Israelites became slaves there. Moses was saved from death as an infant by his mother and sister. As a young man, he struck an Egyptian dead in fury over injustice meted out to the Hebrew slaves. He fled, a murderer.

In the desert where Moses had been hiding for many years, God's call reached him. He was to lead his people to freedom. Uncertain, Moses responded, "But they will never believe me or listen to me. They will say, "The Lord did not appear to you'" (Exodus 4:1). Of course God prevailed in this verbal wrestling match with the man who was to become Israel's greatest leader and friend of God. "There has never yet risen in Israel a prophet like Moses, whom the Lord knew face to face" (Deuteronomy 34:10).

Moses was succeeded by Joshua, warrior and confidant of Moses. In Deuteronomy 31:14 the Lord says to Moses, "Call Joshua and then come and stand in the tent of the presence so that I may give him his commission." Before Moses died he laid hands on Joshua; at that point Joshua was filled with the spirit of wisdom. Not only did he lead the people into the promised land, but he acted as their spiritual leader as well.

Historically it seems that after taking possession of the land, the tribes of Israel, not really united, were governed by judges noted for warring skills and wisdom. When one of the twelve tribes was attacked, some of the neighboring tribes might join the battle. One of the judges, Deborah, was particularly acclaimed for her wisdom (Judges 4). The "raising up" of judges, both women and men, was the Lord's work. The Spirit of the Lord would "wrap the judge round" (Knox translation), inspiring leadership for crisis situations.

When Gideon is called to be a judge, he argues with the Lord, pleading that his clan is the weakest in his tribe, that he is the least in his family (Judges 6:15). After a spectacular victory over their enemies, the people beg Gideon to stay on as their ruler. He insists that only the Lord is ruler of Israel, but later is tempted to power and idolatry (Judges 8:22-27).

In our day, Paddy Chayevsky's play, *Gideon*, performed on stage or public television, provides a fine example of biblical spirituality. A very real Gideon converses with one he knows loves him, a very real God. Their intimacy is a refreshing witness to how God initiates relationship.

The last judge of Israel is the majestic Samuel. He is a kind of circuit rider, moving through the tribes, dispensing justice and speaking on behalf of God.

Samuel's vocation begins with God's calling the boy in the middle of the night. God takes the initiative. "Speak, Lord, your servant is listening" (1 Samuel 3:10-11) is the child's response.

An older Samuel struggled with his people who wanted a king, a permanent ruler over Israel. God was their only king, the one who had led them out of Egypt. God shared feelings of rejection with Samuel, but gave the Israelites Saul. When Samuel approached Saul, the young man protested that his was the smallest tribe and his family the least important in the tribe (1 Samuel 9:21). After Samuel anointed Saul, "God gave Saul a new heart" (1 Samuel 10:10).

Saul's fortunes, despite the new God-given heart, were tied to war. Once, disobedient to the Lord's command, Saul was warned by Samuel: "You have rejected the word of the Lord and therefore the Lord has rejected you as king over Israel" (1 Samuel 15:26). While Saul was still in power, Samuel anointed David, the youngest of his family. Saul's mental disturbances were soothed when the boy David played his harp. Soon the youth became both a threat to the insecure king and a friend to the king's son Jonathan (1 Samuel 18-20).

When David ascended the throne he united the twelve tribes around his new capital city, Jerusalem. The ark of the covenant, a special box fashioned during their forty years of desert wandering, had been captured by the Philistines but recovered by David. So great was the king's joy in bringing this symbol of God's presence to Jerusalem that he danced before the ark as it processed through the Judean hills toward Jerusalem (2 Samuel 6:12-23).

A new promise of God was given David and his descendants through the prophet Nathan (2 Samuel 7:8-16). This covenant was a promise of God's unconditional love.

Nathan later accused king David of terrible sin. David tried to usurp power which belongs only to God. Not only did the king commit adultery with Bathsheba, but he tried to manipulate events to cover up his sin and her pregnancy, eventually causing the death of her husband (2 Samuel 12). Yet before and after his great sin, David is beloved of the Lord.

David's son Solomon also abused power. Injustice, slavery, and murder reigned in the wealthy court of Solomon. Materialism prevailed and God was spurned. After Solomon's death the kingdom united by David was split. The northern ten tribes were called Israel; the southern two tribes were known as Judah.

Some Common Experiences of Leaders

From these thumbnail sketches the reader can see some common threads in the lives of Israel's leaders. Their call to leadership often surprised them, and often they protested that they were too weak, too insignificant to do God's work. It is particularly instructive to know that God chose one murderer, Moses, to lead the exodus from Egypt; another, David, to provide the model of kingship. A number of leaders failed their God: Gideon, Saul, Solomon. God seems to delight in selecting the sinner and the insignificant.

Often these leaders made a covenant with God. Abraham, Moses, and David received promises of the Lord's unswerving fidelity, sealed by a covenant. The great Israelite covenant was the one made at Sinai in which the Lord gave the law to the people through Moses' mediation. If you keep my law, I will be your God, the Lord promised. This covenant was conditional.

Yet God's love remained steadfastly forgiving, always welcoming the sinful. God had rescued the Hebrews from Egypt's oppression, "bearing them up on eagle's wings." They forgot their Redeemer, however, and began to sin. Then some new oppression would call them to their senses. In their desperation they would cry out to God, whose heart would melt. Once again God would save this people, set them free in the open. How fervently they would promise to be faithful to God when their saving was still fresh!

The Jewish Scriptures underscore this dynamic: sin/oppression/cry/deliverance. The people would sin, then experience some pain, famine, defeat, oppression. They would call out to God and God would faithfully set them free again.

Deliverance, liberation is an important experience of the people. God's mighty devotion to them in the exodus experience is continually recalled. They remind each other—in worship, such as the feast of Passover, in the psalms, in their stories.

The exodus is the touchstone against which other manifestations of God are measured. One manifestation of God's faithful presence was the ark of the covenant. It contained the tablets of the law and later some manna and the rod of Aaron. The ark was housed in a tent called the tabernacle, literally the tent of presence. The Israelites' God was free to pack up this tent and move on. The God who set free was eminently free, a tenting God.

Another manifestation of God's presence to Israel was the law, the Torah. Many of us were taught that the Jewish law applied to us Christians. We may still be enslaved by legalism, flooded by guilt if we break a law. Jesus in the Gospels railed against the legalism of the Pharisees, accusing them of making the law a burden. To the Jew who loved the law, however, it was life, a reminder of God's covenanting love and continual liberation.

Often the law is linked with the prophets: "the law and the prophets." Prophecy is yet another manifestation of God's presence in the community. Some of Israel's leaders were designated prophets; for example: Moses, Deborah, Samuel, Saul. They were God's spokespersons, calling the people back to covenant, promising God's liberation. We will explore prophecy and the works of some of the prophets in the next chapter.

Guided Prayer

Abraham

Genesis 15:1-7

> The word of the Lord came to Abram in a vision: "Do not be afraid, Abram. I am your shield. I will make your reward abundant."
>
> Abram replied, "O Lord God, what good will your gifts do me if I have no child.... You have given me no offspring.... How can I be sure?"
>
> Then God took Abram out and said, "Look up

and count the stars in the sky if you can. That is
how many your descendants will be."

So Abram put his faith in the Lord. God cred-
ited that to him as righteousness.

Then God said, "I am the Lord who brought you
up from the land of the Chaldeans in order to give
you this land as your own."

Relating with someone means being called to trust,
to risk, to change, to journey. Remember your relationships and your growth in trust. On the other hand, when
have you felt that all is lost? What comfort or promise
have you felt at that time? "Lord, how can I be sure...?"
Tell God how you feel. Ask for the gift of trusting God's
faithful care for you.

Joseph

Read Genesis 39-45 for background; Psalm 105:16-21

God called down a famine on the land; it destroyed all their crops.

Then God sent a man to go before them: Joseph:
sold as a slave.

They had bound him tight, bound him with
chains.

Then Joseph's word came to pass and the word
of God proved him true (both correct and faithful).

Pharaoh sent and released him; the ruler set
Joseph free, making him lord of his household,
steward of all Pharaoh's possessions.

Out of slavery comes freedom. Remember some of
your sufferings, especially any injustices you have suffered. Discuss them and your feelings about them with
the Lord. Ask for God's continuing healing and growth
in hope that out of death will come life.

Moses

Exodus 33:17-23; 34:5-6

God said to Moses, "I will do what you want because you have found favor with me. You are my intimate friend."

Then Moses said: "Let me see your glory."

God responded, "I will make all my beauty pass before you and I will pronounce my name. I show favor to whom I want and grant mercy to those I will. You may not, however, see my face, for no one can see me face to face and still live. Here, near me, is a place in this rock. When my glory passes by you I will set you in this cleft in the rock. I will cover you with my hand till I have passed by. Then I will take my hand away so that you may see my back; but my face you shall not see."

Coming down in a cloud, the Lord stood with Moses and proclaimed this name: "The Lord, the Lord, a God compassionate and gracious, slow to anger and abounding in kindness and faithfulness...."

When we read this conversation, we are participating in it. We are asking to see God. What name does God reveal to you? Ask where in your life you can find the face, the glory, the beauty of the Lord. Then sit quietly and try to listen.

Exodus 15:20-21; 16:2-3; 17:1-4

When the waters flowed back on Pharaoh and his charioteers, the prophetess Miriam, sister of Moses and Aaron, took a tambourine and led all the women of Israel with tambourines and dancing. They sang: "Sing to the Lord, for God is triumphant! Horse and chariot God casts into the sea!..."

Out in the desert, however, the whole community of Israel murmured against Moses and Aaron. They said, "Would that we had died in the land of Egypt! There at least we sat by the fleshpots and ate all the bread we wanted. But you led us into this desert so the whole community can die of starvation!"

The whole community moved by stages as the Lord directed. When they camped at Rephidim there was no water to drink. Again they murmured, quarreling with Moses: "Give us water to drink."

Moses answered, "Why quarrel with me and put God to the test?"

In their thirst they grumbled, "Why did you ever make us leave Egypt? Was it just to have us die here?..."

So Moses cried out, "Lord, what shall I do with this people? Soon they will stone me!"

Notice how Moses and Miriam are closely involved with the people. To be close to the Lord involves us with God's community. What is the rhythm in your life between prayer and service of others, the dynamic of action for people and contemplation of the Lord? Instead of thinking about it, philosophizing about it, ask the Lord to teach you. How does God want your spiritual life and your family life, your work and your church service to interact? Sit quietly and try to listen.

Joshua

Excerpts from Joshua 24

Joshua gathered all the tribes of Israel at Shechem, calling forth their elders, leaders, judges and officers. When they stood before God, Joshua spoke to all the people....

"Thus says the Lord: Once you crossed the Jordan river and came to Jericho, I delivered the defenders of the city into your power.... I gave you a land you had not plowed, cities you had not built, vineyards and olive groves you did not plant."

Joshua said, "Reverence the Lord. Serve God completely and sincerely. Cast out the gods your ancestors served beyond the river and in Egypt and serve the Lord. If you do not want to serve the Lord, decide today whom you will serve. As for me and my household, we will serve the Lord."

The people responded, "Far be it from us to forsake the Lord to worship other gods. It was the Lord who brought us and our ancestors out of Egypt, out of slavery.... Therefore we too will serve the Lord."

Joshua said in reply, "You may not be able to serve the Lord, for God is a holy God, a jealous God...."

But the people all promised, "We will serve the Lord and obey God's voice."

Notice how before Joshua challenges the people to make a choice, he calls to their memory the saving actions of the Lord on their behalf, a sign to them of how God loves them. The people respond, but Joshua confronts them. You are sinners, he tells them in effect. Only if we really know the Lord's kindness to us have we the courage to admit our sin. Only if we admit our sin can we repent. But notice that in bringing us to repentance God, like Joshua, first reminds us how dearly we have been loved. Speak with the Lord about this dynamic of God's love/your repentance and how it deepens your closeness with each other.

Gideon

Read Judges 6-8 for background; Judges 6:12-18

> While Gideon was working, the angel of the Lord appeared to him and said, "The Lord is with you, champion."

> "My Lord," Gideon addressed the angel, "if the Lord is with us why has all this (attack from the enemy) happened to us? Where are God's wonderful works of which our ancestors told us, how the Lord brought us up from Egypt? See, now the Lord has abandoned us and delivered us to our enemy, the Midianites."

> The Lord turned to Gideon and said, "Go with all your strength and save Israel from the power of Midian. It is I who am sending you."

> Gideon replied, "Please, Lord, how can I save Israel? My family is least in the tribe of Manasseh, and I am the least in my father's household."

> "I shall be with you and you will cut down the Midianites," answered the Lord.

What do you notice in this encounter? How do you feel about Gideon's relationship with the Lord? Would you like to be so honest with God? Tell God how you feel and what you want in your relationship.

David

Read, for background, 2 Samuel 11 and 12, one of the literary gems in the Bible. 2 Samuel 11:26-27; 12:1-8, 13

> When Bathsheba heard that her husband had died, she mourned. But when she had finished, David sent for her and brought her into his house. She became his wife and the baby born to them was

a son. But the Lord was not pleased with what David had done.

The Lord sent the prophet Nathan to King David. Nathan said, "Judge this case for me. Once there were two men in a town, one rich and the other poor. The rich man had flocks and herds in abundance but the poor man had only one small ewe lamb. He fed her and she grew up with his children, even sleeping in his bosom; she was like a daughter to the poor man. One day the rich man entertained a visitor but did not want to take anything from his own flock to prepare a meal. So instead he took the little ewe lamb from the poor man in order to serve a meal to his visitor."

David became very angry, "As the Lord lives, the man who has done this should die! He must restore this lamb fourfold because he has had no pity."

Then Nathan said to David, "That man is you! Thus says the Lord to you: I anointed you king of Israel, rescuing you from Saul, giving you his house and his wives to be your own. I gave you the house of Israel and of Judah, and if this were not enough, I would have given you more...."

Then David cried to Nathan, "I have sinned against the Lord."

Nathan responded, "The Lord has forgiven you your sin, you shall not die...."

"Had this not been enough, I would have added other favors as great." God reminds David of all the gifts the king has received. Why, the Lord asks, must David take matters into his own hands? How does our desire and often our attempt to control things, people, our own lives usurp God's power? Talk with God about control

and surrender, about your creaturehood and God's lord-
ship. Then try to listen.

Exercises

Read more extensively the chapters describing your favorite Israelite leader. What qualities of leadership do you
find in him or her? What qualities are needed in our church
and political leaders today? Ask members of your group
to reflect on their own leadership abilities. Where, when,
how does each lead? Discuss. Be open to feedback from the
group should they affirm your abilities.

In the privacy of your room, remember God's presence.
Would you dare to dance for God as David did?

Pay attention to all the "shoulds" in your life on any given
day. Write the times you acted, thought, felt a certain way
because you "should." Where do these "shoulds" come
from? Parents, teachers, preachers? The Jewish law?
Jesus? What do you want to do with these "shoulds"?
What does God want you to do with them?

Which leader in the Jewish Scriptures do you like best?
Why? Which one challenges you most? Why? Share with
your group.

4. The Lovers

God's love is a fire, alluring and passionate. How can the Lord communicate so much tenderness to the chosen people? God initiates a very intimate relationship with those we name prophets. Prophets come so close to the mind and heart of God that they dare to speak the Lord's mind. More importantly perhaps, they voice what is in God's heart. Prophecy, the Jewish theologian Rabbi Abraham Heschel teaches, is the voice which God lends to the silent agony of the poor.

Prophets speak the word of God to the people. That word, we learn from Hebrews 4:12-13, is a two-edged sword; it can penetrate the most hidden motives of our hearts. The word spoken by the prophets cuts to the core of a sinning people. This prophetic word warns, pleads, challenges, critiques. The other edge of the sword wielded by the prophets is silken soft, a word to soothe a people who are oppressed by enemies or by their own unjust rulers. Prophets comfort or challenge, criticize or console.

Contrary to popular belief, prophets do not make specific predictions of the future. This is an important understanding lest we trivialize the urgent message of the prophets, likening them to fortune tellers. God does not offer a crystal ball to the prophets but rather an intimate relationship with all its power, peace, pain and joy. Prophets speak only out of their deep communion with God.

One of the ways in which the early Christians used the Jewish Scriptures, such as Peter's speech on Pentecost, was to find in them verification of all God had done in the death and resurrection of Jesus. The Jews believed that anyone who hung on a tree was cursed by God (Deuteronomy 21:23): therefore Jesus, hung on the cross, was cursed by God. The first Christians had to "prove" that Jesus was, on the contrary, blessed by God.

To prove that God vindicated Jesus instead of cursing him, they would use the authority of the Jewish Scriptures. They would have seen in the Suffering Servant song of Isaiah 53, for example, proof that God lets the Servant suffer but finally vindicates him. It was a short step for Christians to imagine that Isaiah had seen into the future and could predict Jesus' torture and death.

To make such an application of a particular Scripture passage to a particular person or situation was a common practice among Jews in Jesus' time. This kind of Scripture interpretation is called *pesher*. It is still a practice among some Christians, who once were certain that parts of the Book of Revelation applied to Hitler, or communism's rise, or Russia's demise.

The world has not ended, however, nor is God deceiving us. In our attempt to pin God down, to become secure by knowing the future, we are using Scripture for purposes never intended by its authors. Jesus claims that even he does not know the day nor the hour.

Prophecy is the voice God has lent to our silent agony. Prophets are mightily concerned with justice, with politics, with widows and orphans. Prophecy springs from identification with the suffering of the people. Prophecy is especially the record of the prophets' identifying with the suffering of God. Prophets are so united with God that they share the very feelings, mind and word of God.

Amos and Hosea

Amos and Hosea are two prophets who spoke to the northern kingdom of Israel in the decades before that kingdom fell in 721 B.C. Amos is a shepherd who protests his prophetic vocation. He does not want to be a prophet. Nonetheless he shares God's passion for justice.

Greek philosophers taught that the supreme characteristic of God was apathy—literally *a-patheia* in Greek— absence of passion. Their God was without passion. Not so for the Jews. Their God was full of passion. God's hatred expressed by Amos (i.e., 5:21; 6:8) shows God's passionate revulsion for pomp, arrogance, religiosity, wealth, trampling on the rights of the defenseless. God's anger is with those who offend the poor (Amos 8), and through Amos God roars that anger like a lion (Amos 1:2; 3:8). Amos envisions a rolling river of justice, a powerful image in such an arid land as Israel. This justice which the prophet proclaims so vehemently is not legal so much as communal, springing from covenant relationship. Our acts of injustice are a betrayal of our God, who is justice.

No prophet understands betrayal so well as Hosea. This prophet, on God's instruction, marries a woman who is unfaithful. So deep and lasting is Hosea's love that he cannot face separation. When she runs off with other lovers, he keeps wooing her back to him, hoping that her fidelity might some day match his own.

Hosea's call to prophecy is an inner identification of his love and fidelity with God's own faithful love for Israel. Hosea's fury at the injustice of his wife's betrayals does not harden his heart against her, any more than

God's anger at our betrayals leads God to abandon us. Rather Hosea's forgiveness wipes out her past sin, just as *hesed* and *'emet* continually renew our intimacy with God.

Hosea's whole married life, his children, his family become a symbol through which God speaks faithful love. Prophets speak not only in words, but often in actions as well.

The Jews had a hard time believing that God's love could be so foolish as Hosea's. This book was put in and taken out of the canon of the Jewish Scriptures for centuries. Finally in the thirteenth century after Christ, the rabbis let it stand, a witness to just how unconditional is God's love for us.

Isaiah

The prophecy of Isaiah was compiled over centuries. The original prophet Isaiah was an aristocrat from Jerusalem, called in a majestic vision of God. "Whom shall I send?" cries the Lord. Isaiah eagerly replies, "Send me" (Isaiah 6:9). From his prophecy, comforting the people, sprang a hope for a Messiah from King David's line, an ideal "Prince of Peace."

Like other prophets, Isaiah does not only use words to communicate God's messages of promise and doom. He also uses the prophetic gesture, a bodily sign. For example, Isaiah, in a prophetic gesture, walks naked in Jerusalem for three years to symbolize how Assyria will strip the nations naked (Isaiah 20).

Two centuries later (538 B.C.), near the end of the Babylonian exile when the cream of Israelite society had been carried off in slavery, more material was added to the prophecy of Isaiah. Chapters 40-55 are called Deutero (or Second) Isaiah.

The theology of this prophet focuses on a new age dawning. Through Second Isaiah God promises a new exodus. God delivers Israel again, this time from bondage in Babylon.

At this point in their history, Israel comes to know God anew. Not only is God Savior, the primal experience of the Israelite community, set free in the open Sinai wilderness. Now, the people experience God as Creator of all. Salvation is understood as universal, possible for all nations.

Some scholars attribute Chapters 56-66 to Third Isaiah. This material was written after the exile. Third Isaiah focuses on the rebuilding of Jerusalem, the new temple (62:1-7). The day of the Lord, once a frightening threat of God's anger (Amos 8:9), becomes a light, a time of gathering all peoples home to God (Isaiah 60).

Jeremiah

The Book of Jeremiah is the self-disclosure of a passionate lover of his Lord. Living near Jerusalem with his priestly family, Jeremiah experiences his prophetic vocation in 626 B.C. He prophesies right up to the destruction of Jerusalem by the Babylonians.

Like Hosea's, Jeremiah's life is to be a prophetic message. He is to remain celibate as a prophetic sign that chaos will befall the people and their children (16:1-4). Unlikely, unwilling, still Jeremiah served the word of God for forty-six years. He was exhausted. Even God fails him. The prophet complains to God:

Why then is my pain unending, my wound desperate and incurable? You are to me like a brook that is not to be trusted, whose waters fail (15:18).

Jeremiah identifies with God, particularly feeling God's pain (2:5; 14:17). God even feels homeless among the people, in the promised land (14:8-9).

"I am full of the wrath of God," Jeremiah asserts (6:11). God's word is like a fire in his heart (20:7-12), burning him up, burning him out. The length of his mission, the intensity of his passions, constant persecution wear Jeremiah down. Both mental and physical punishment are his (18:23; Chapters 36 and 38).

Out of Jeremiah's experience with God and people grows the promise of a new covenant (31:31-34), which God will make with a people of circumcised hearts (4:4). Out of the prophet's experience with one of the few good kings from David's line, Josiah, comes Jeremiah's belief that to know the Lord is to do justice (22:13-16). To know, or be united with God, is to share God's life of justice in action.

Justice is a chief theme of all these prophetic lovers. If we say, however, that the God of the Old Testament is a God of justice while the God of the New Testament is a God of mercy, we perpetuate an ancient Christian heresy. The God of the Jewish Scriptures is indeed a God of mercy. Mercy is often the translation of *hesed* which is most characteristic of the God of Israel. Moreover, God in the New Testament is a God of justice. Justice is characteristic of Jesus who himself hungers and thirsts for justice (Matthew 5:6).

Justice in Hebrew and Greek, the biblical languages, means righteousness or holiness. The prophets who preached social justice received their words of justice from the source of all holiness, God. For us to know the Lord, to be intimately united with our God in our time and political situation is to do God's own justice.

Guided Prayer

Amos

Amos 4:6-9; 12-13

Listen to our God lamenting, crying out of the deep anger of being betrayed:

> In all your cities I have cleaned your teeth free of food, I have made food scarce in all your homes. Yet you did not return to me.

> Though I withheld rain, sending rain on one city and not on another, watering one field while another was parched, though you staggered to find water which did not quench your thirst, yet you did not return to me.

> I struck you with scorching wind, letting locusts devour your gardens and vineyards, your fig trees and olive trees. Yet you did not return to me....

> So now I will deal with you in my own way. Prepare to meet your God, my people! I formed the mountains and created the wind, yet I speak to you. I am the one who fashioned the dawn and the darkness. I stride above the earth and the Lord is my name!

When have you, like God, felt so betrayed, so angry? Has one you loved ever shunned you? Ask God to let you remember the pain of it so that you may feel-with God, feel what our turning away causes God to "feel."

To feel-with God is to offer compassion (*com* in Latin is "with" and passion in Latin means to suffer). Scripture invites us to suffer with God. Not because suffering is good. Because we want to be with God, sharing on a deep level what God feels.

Amos 7:1-6

> God showed me, Amos, a locust swarm. While the locust were devouring the land, I cried out: Forgive, O Lord God! How can we stand? We are so very small!
>
> So God repented of this destruction. It shall not be, said the Lord God.
>
> Then the Lord showed me judgment by fire. It had devoured the abyss and was destroying the land when I cried: Stop, O Lord God! How can we stand? We are so small!
>
> So again God repented. This also shall not be, said the Lord God.

When we feel that God is angry, we tend to cringe. We need instead to lower our proud heads and admit, "We are so small." Ask God to do justice on behalf of the small people, the helpless and voiceless. Then ask God to repent of any anger which our hardened or arrogant hearts may arouse, and to forgive.

Hosea

From Chapters 1 and 2

> God said to Hosea: Go, take a prostitute as a wife, for this land has turned to prostitution. So he took Gomer, and she bore him a son.
>
> The Lord said to Hosea: Give him the name Jezreel. Then Hosea's wife bore again and God said: Give this daughter the name Lo-ruhama, meaning she who is not pitied, for I no longer feel pity for the house of Israel. Finally, Gomer bore a son and God said: Call him Lo-ammi, meaning not my people, because you are not my people and I will not be your God.

The Lord continued: Protest against your mother for she is not my wife and I am not her husband. Let her throw her adultery far from herself or I will strip her naked.... I will make of her a desert, reduce her to arid land and will have no pity on her children.

She replied: I will go after my lovers who give me bread and water, wool and flax, oil and drink.

She does not know, says the Lord, that it was I who gave her grain and wine and oil, an abundance of silver and gold.... I will bring an end to her joy, her feasts, her sabbaths and solemnities. When she adorned herself with jewels and went after her lovers, she forgot me, says the Lord. So I will hedge her in.... When she runs after her lovers she shall not find them.... Then she will say: "I will go back to my first husband, for it was better with me than now."

So I will allure her, leading her into the desert and thus speak to her heart. I will give her vineyards and she shall respond to me as in the days of her youth when she came up from Egypt. On that day, says the Lord, she shall call me her husband.... I will make a covenant.... I will espouse you to myself forever, in justice and love and mercy. I will espouse you in faithfulness and you shall know the Lord. I will have pity on Lo-ruhama, and I will say to Lo-ammi "You are my people," and he shall say: "My God!"

What are the "corn, new wine and oil" in your life? What good gifts has the Lord lavished on you? Sit quietly and ask the Spirit to show you God's gifts. Let your gifts just bubble up from deep within you. How do you feel about these gifts?

Hosea 6:1-3

> When they are afflicted they shall look for me, saying: Come, let us return to the Lord, for if God has struck, so God will heal us and bind up our wounds. The Lord will revive us after two days. On the third day our God will raise us up and we shall live in the Lord's presence. Let us know, let us strive to know the Lord. As certain as the dawn is our God's coming, shining like the light of day. God comes to us like the rain, like spring rain which waters the earth.

When do you feel that God has torn you? How has God healed you? Do you feel healed? Tell God what you still need.

Hosea 6:4-6

> God responds: What can I do with you, Ephraim, or with you Judah? Your devotion is like a morning mist, like the dew which quickly fades away. For this reason I smote you through the prophets and struck you with the words of my mouth. For it is love that I desire, not sacrifice. I want you to know me, not offer holocausts.

Ask for the gift of steady faithfulness that won't vanish like the morning mist. Ask that you might know (remember that "know" means be attached to) and trust God.

Hosea 14:5-9

> I will heal the sin of my people and I will love them freely, for my anger is turned away from them. I shall be like a dew to Israel; my people shall blossom like the lily.... Their splendor shall be like

that of the olive tree, with a fragrance like the cedar of Lebanon. They shall dwell in shade and raise grain, blossoming like the vine, famous as the wine from Lebanon. What more has Ephraim to do with false gods? If once I humbled my people, now I prosper them. I am like a green cypress tree for them. Because of me they bear fruit.

Our God is a father, a healer, a lover, a dew, a sheltering cypress tree. What have you learned about who God is from Hosea? How has this prophet helped you to know/be attached to the Lord?

Isaiah

Isaiah 1:11-13, 17-19

Hear the word of the Lord, cries Isaiah:

What do I care for the number of your sacrifices? I have had enough of your holocausts, fat and blood of calves and lambs and goats. These give me no joy. When you come to visit me, who wants these things from you? Do not trample my courts, do not bring worthless gifts. I hate your incense, your new moons, sabbaths and festivals....

Learn to do good. Act justly toward the wronged, listen to the orphan's cry and defend the widow. Come now, let us argue this out and set it right. Even if your sins are as scarlet, they will become white as snow; though they are crimson, they will become white as wool. If you are willing and obey, you shall eat the good fruits of the land.

Here is the prophet's understanding of true morality; it is Jesus' idea too. Who are the wronged, the orphans, the widows in your life? What people need you? How do you respond to them? Talk with the Lord about your response. Ask for the gifts of compassion and justice.

Isaiah 43:1-5, 12

> Thus says the Lord, who created you, who formed you. My people, do not be afraid for I have redeemed you. I have called you by name and you belong to me. If you pass through raging waters, I will be with you; you shall not drown. If you walk through fire you shall not be burned. I am the Lord, your God, your savior.
>
> I give whole worlds for you, because you are precious to me and glorious, because I love you. Do not be afraid for I am with you...I hold you and no one can snatch you from my hand.

How do you feel about this message? Ask God for the gift of trust, that you may really believe and rejoice in all God's delight in you.

Isaiah 46:3-5

> Hear me, all who remain of the house of Israel. I have carried you since your birth, borne your burden since your infancy. Even in your old age I will be faithful. When your hair is gray I will carry you. Who is like me?

Who is like me? the Lord asks. God carries us, bears our burdens. This is how Isaiah describes the God with whom he relates. What is your image of God? Sit quietly and try to listen to the Spirit teach you who God is for you.

Isaiah 49:8-16

> Thus says the Lord: On the day of salvation I help you, restoring the land, saying to prisoners: Come out!...saying to those in darkness: Come forth! All along the way they shall find food. They

shall neither hunger nor thirst, nor shall wind or sun scorch them. One who loves them leads them, and guides them to springs of water.

I will cut a road through the mountains, making the highways smooth.... Break into song, you mountains, for the Lord comforts the people and shows kindness to the afflicted.

The people of Zion say: The Lord has forsaken me; my God has forgotten me.

Can a mother forget her baby, or abandon the child of her womb? Yet even if she forget, I will never forget you. I have carved you on the palms of my hands. I have written your name and you are before me always.

One who loves you will lead you. Ask again for trust. When have you ever felt forgotten by the Lord? Talk about it in this time of prayer, even if you still feel angry with God. Again ask to trust that you are unique and special to God.

Isaiah 50:4

The Lord God has given me a skillful word, that I might know how to speak to the weary a word of comfort in the morning. Morning after morning God opens my ear that I might hear and learn.

All Christians are invited to come close to God, to learn the mind and heart of God, to be so close that we dare to speak God's word of comfort and/or challenge. Whether to console or to critique? Before offering a prophetic word, pray the serenity prayer:

O God, grant me the serenity to accept the things I cannot change; the courage to change the things I can; and the wisdom to know the difference.

Isaiah 55:1-3, 7-12

> All you who are thirsty, come to the water. All you who are poor, come and receive grain. Come without money and drink wine and milk. Why spend your money for what never satisfies you? If you pay attention to me, you shall eat well, delighting as at a banquet.
>
> Come to me, the Lord says, and pay attention; listen that you may have life.... Let the wicked turn to me for mercy, for I am generous and forgiving. For my thoughts are not your thoughts nor are my ways your ways. As far as the heavens are above the earth, so far are my ways beyond your ways, my thoughts beyond your thoughts. Just as rain and snow come from the heavens, watering the earth, bringing forth fruit, giving seed to those who sow and bread to those who eat, so my word will not return empty. It goes forth from my mouth and accomplishes what I want. As for you, you shall go forward in joy, and in peace you shall return.

Read this slowly, and remember that the word of the Lord does what it says; nourishes, calls you back, penetrates the earthiness of you, causes rejoicing and peace. What lines make you feel or want something? Express those desires and feelings to the Lord.

Isaiah 62:1-5

> For Zion's sake I will not be silent, until Jerusalem's vindication shines like the dawn. Nations shall look on your triumph. You shall be called a new name, proclaimed by the mouth of your Lord. You shall be a precious crown in God's hand. Never again shall people call you "Abandoned" or your land "Desolate." For the Lord delights in you, makes your land beloved. As a young

man marries a virgin, so shall your builder marry you; as a bridegroom rejoices in his bride, so your God shall rejoice in you.

The word of the Lord does what it says. You are being held as precious in the hand of the Lord. You are never forsaken. You are the Lord's delight, God's own beloved. You are the cause of the Lord's rejoicing, even as this word is spoken to you today. Ask to believe that this living word makes all this a reality for right now. How do you feel about what God is doing for you, with you, not because you are good but because God is good? Share those feelings with God.

Jeremiah

Jeremiah 1:4-10

The word of the Lord came to me like this: Before I fashioned you in your mother's womb I knew you; before you were born I consecrated you. I appointed you a prophet.

O Lord God, I said. I do not know how to speak. I am just a child.

The Lord answered me: Do not say, I am too young. You will go to whomever I send you; whatever I tell you, you will speak. Do not be afraid, for I am with you.

Then the Lord touched my mouth, saying: See, I put my words in your mouth...to root up and to tear down, to destroy and demolish, to build up and to plant.

Do you ever argue with God? About what? If not, why not? When you tell God your limitations and God tells you differently, can you hear your Lord? Perhaps God speaks through your friends who affirm you and your gifts. Are you afraid to be chosen by the Lord for some further task? As freely as Jeremiah did, discuss these fears with God.

Jeremiah 31:31-34; 32:40-41

>The days are coming, says the Lord, when I will make a new covenant, not like the covenant I made with their ancestors the day I took them by the hand to lead them out of Egypt. They broke that covenant....

>With this covenant I will place my law deep within them, writing it upon their hearts. I will be their God and they shall be my people. They will no longer need anyone to teach them about me, for they shall know me. From the least to the greatest, all shall know me....

>I will make an everlasting covenant with them, promising always to do good for them. I will put awe for me in their hearts so they will never be separated from me. I will delight in doing good for them. I will replant them firmly in this land with all my heart.

A new covenant is promised. Write your own covenant with the Lord. How do you address God? What does the Lord promise you? What name does God call you? What do you promise? How do you feel? Ask, simply, what God thinks of your desires. Does the Spirit inspire you to make any changes in your proposed covenant? Listen.

Every time we celebrate Eucharist we renew this covenant, a new covenant in Christ Jesus. Next time, at Eucharist, hear God's promise and renew your own pledge.

Jeremiah 4:19; 20:7-9; 23:9; 23:28-29

>My heart, my heart! How I suffer! My heart

beats wildly. I cannot keep silent for I have heard the sound of the trumpet, the alarms for war.

You seduced me, Lord, and I let myself be seduced. You were too strong for me and you won. I am the scorn of people; they mock me all day long. When I try to speak I must cry out; violence is my message. The word of the Lord brings me mocking all day long. I tell myself: I will not mention God again, I will speak the Lord's name no more. Then the word becomes like a fire blazing in my heart, deep in my bones. I am exhausted trying to hold this word back, yet I cannot bear it.

My heart within me is broken and all my bones tremble. I am like one drunk because of the Lord, because of God's holy word.

Let the prophet who dreams tell the dream, the prophet who has my word speak faithfully. The Lord says: My word is like a fire, like a hammer which shatters rocks.

Can you, called, chosen and anointed as a prophet at your baptism, in any way identify with Jeremiah as he wrestles with his call to speak the word of challenge and comfort? For whom, to whom do you speak this word? This is the mission the Lord gives you. How do you feel about it? Discuss these things with the one who puts this fiery word in your mouth.

Jeremiah 8:18, 21-23

My grief cannot be healed. My heart within me is weak.... I am broken by the ruin of my people, terror seizes me. There is no balm in Gilead, no healing there.... My head feels like a spring of water, my eyes are fountains of tears, that I might weep night and day over the slaying of my people.

Do you feel deeply about people? Which ones? Why? Is anything blocking you from caring more consistently? Can you get angry with those you care about? Feel tenderness? Talk with the Lord about the whole range of feelings in your various relationships and ask for the gift of compassion, the ability to feel-with.

Jeremiah 3:12-13; 8:5-6

Return, rebel people, says the Lord. I will not stay angry with you, for I am full of kindness. My wrath shall not last forever. Only know your guilt. Acknowledge that you have turned from the Lord, running here and there to strange gods, not paying attention to my voice.

Why do these people turn away so stubbornly? Why do they cling to their idols and refuse to come back to me? I listen closely, but what they say is not true. No one repents, crying: What have I done?

How capable are you of admitting your creaturehood, your sinfulness? How capable are you of forgiving yourself your own humanity? How capable is the Lord of forgiving your most gross rebellion? Ask to trust this unconditional love, to trust that God loves you just the way you are.

Jeremiah 30:17-19; 31:7-14

I will restore you to health and heal your wounds, says the Lord.... I will restore your tents...and build again a city on a hill....

Then shall they sing hymns of praise, with laughter. I will increase them. They will no longer be tiny, for I will glorify them.

How able are you to receive from other people (favors, gifts, help with a task, etc.)? How able are you to accept kindness from others? from the Lord? If you really allow God to heal you and to whole you, what will be different in your life?

Jeremiah 29:11

> My plans for you are plans of peace, not disaster. I have reserved for you a future full of hope.

What good news God speaks through this usually mournful prophet! Who can believe it when so often we were told that our pain, loss and suffering "must be God's holy will"? Here is God's will, God's passionate desire: our peace.

Peace in Hebrew is *shalom*. *Shalom* also means wholeness, healing, integrity. God hungers for our wholeness. God never plans or wants disaster. In an imperfect world, always groaning toward fuller freedom, the earth and we ourselves may experience labor pangs, Paul writes (Romans 8:19-25); but we hope, for life is being born.

Exercises

Our baptism makes us prophets, a royal priesthood. That means that God has given each of us a prophetic vocation through baptism. Remember and share a time when you experienced something bigger, someone greater than yourself taking you over. Remember when you were given an appropriate word or gesture of comfort or challenge for someone else. When has God given you a word to comfort or challenge your family or community?

Listen to Handel's "Messiah," so deeply rooted in passages from Isaiah. Many people are familiar only with the Christmas sections. The second part of it hymns Jesus' death and resurrection. If this music moves you, invite someone to listen to it with you. Let it be a time of prayer when the prophetic word sinks into you and accomplishes what God wants in your listening heart.

Lovers identify with each other. The prophets identify with God. Remember being in love. Take five minutes of silent remembering in your group. Share the experience, feelings, memories in a faith sharing style; no verbal comments after each one speaks. Then take another five minutes of silence together and feel that "in love" experience with God. Conclude without words in the group but with a sign, a hug of peace.

Besides the poignant picture of God as a passionate, wronged lover, Hosea offers a picture of God as parent, mother or father, teaching a child to walk (Hosea 11:3-4). The northern kingdom, called Ephraim here, was called out of Egypt at the time of the exodus. God speaks through the prophet:

It was I who taught Ephraim to walk, I who had taken them in my arms. They did not know that I... led them with bonds of love, that I had lifted them like a little child to my cheek, that I had bent down to feed them.

In a role-play, let two people in the group act out their response to their child's first steps. The group watches faces, eyes, body language of the two "parents" during the role-play. The imaginary baby begins to toddle, then falls. How do the "parents" respond?

After the role-play let the "parents" report their own feelings, then receive feedback from the group. How do the observers feel? Have any in the group ever felt that, as they learned to walk in Christian life, God was waiting for their first misstep, their first fall, to swoop down on them with hell-fire? Discuss. How can we be healed of that image of God? How can we be instruments of healing for others? Discuss.

Many lyrics of modern hymns are taken from the prophets. Pay attention to the sources of next Sunday's hymns and share with your group one or two of your favorite hymns based an the prophetic writings.

5. The Psalms

The word "psalms" means praises. In the one hundred and fifty psalms recorded in our Scriptures, however, we find not only praises but laments, thanks, curses, desires, joys, sufferings. Every emotion is proclaimed to God, every curse and blessing is spoken in God's hearing. Psalms are prayers of the heart, acknowledgments that God permeates each of us at the core (Latin: *cor*, heart). Our intense and intimate relationship is expressed in the psalms in a variety of ways.

Scholars classify psalms in several ways. Probably the most problematic type is the cursing psalm. Historical psalms offer an excellent way to share faith, telling the community how God has worked in our personal and peoples' history. Laments, complaining psalms, make up one-third of the Psalter, the book of 150 psalms. Of course, there are also psalms of praise and thanksgiving.

Scholars debate whether the psalms are written for communities or for individuals. Because of my over-arching belief that Scripture is a community expression of faith, I hold that all psalms are communitarian, even though sometimes cast in the first person and revealing most private sentiments.

Psalms as Poetry

Scholars do agree that psalms are poetry. Hebrew poetry is characterized by parallelism. One of the ways we can understand the meaning of Hebrew words is to pay attention to the parallelism in Hebrew poetry. For example, the psalmist prayed:

Bless the Lord, O my soul

And all my being, bless God's holy name (Ps 103).

We can diagram the parallelism like this:

Bless the Lord, O my soul

And all my being, bless God's holy name.

"Soul" in the first line is in a parallel position with "all my being." "Soul" is an English translation, a western concept. Hebrew did not have a word for "soul." But we know by parallelism that the psalmist meant the whole being of a person.

Blessing the Lord, the parallel construction indicates, means the same as blessing God's name. Hebrews believed that the person was present in his or her name.

Sometimes the parallel synonyms do not form a cross (chiasm) as in the example above. Another kind of parallel construction is, for example:

Come! Let us raise a joyful song / to the Lord

a shout of triumph/to the Rock of our salvation (Ps 95)

From the parallelism of the phrases in the second half of each line, we now know what it means for the Lord to be Lord: it is to be a rock for us, the very steadiness of our salvation.

I would also encourage you, especially in praying the psalms, to look at various translations, if such are available to you. For example, in the opening verses of Psalm 103, used as the example above, according to the *New English Bible*, we read, not "all my being" but "my innermost heart, bless God's holy name." A synonym for soul in this translation is "innermost heart." Using a variety of translations in your group can increase your appreciation of the rich depth of meaning in Hebrew poetry.

Cursing Psalms

Some people think that appreciation of the psalms can be marred by the inclusion of cursing psalms in the Psalter. Why so much attention to enemies? Throughout Church history these enemies have often been spiritualized into the enemies of the spiritual life, especially vices. Today's liturgists have removed cursing psalms from the Divine Office.

Let me make a case for cursing our enemies, always realizing that with God there are no wrong emotions, no negative emotions. We are as God created us—capable of hatred, jealousy, despair—good. Every emotion is God's gift to us. Cursing psalms can give us a chance to express some painful emotions in a wholesome way.

There is a personal reason to use cursing psalms. Violence and hatred of enemies, fury and desire for vindication, are all important aspects of being human. To deny these emotions is to repress a part of our wholesome self. Repressing them insures that these same emotions *will* find means for asserting themselves, but in covert, twisted ways.

God asks us to feel all the parts of our self, and to acknowledge the Creator of these emotions. To face them is also to face God, their originator. We are created good.

Then God invites us to pray with these passions. God wants to hear and receive our expression of them in prayer. God knows and understands that we hate and want revenge and are consumed by jealousy. Even God is called a jealous God. Why should we not want with all our heart, as our desiring but frustrated God wants? That is all jealousy is. So we pour out our desires and frustrations, our jealousies, hate, violence to God and we call these outpourings "the cursing psalms." God is not ashamed of our feelings. Emotions are not sinful but signals, God's gifts to us. How better to work through these passions but with God?

Secondly, our call to social justice can lead us to curse on behalf of the helpless, to give voice to the silent agony of the poor in our passionate prayer. Through the 1971 Synod of Bishops, we were alerted to injustice in the world. There are incredible enemies at work against you and me, and we are middle-class members of the first world! Structures of government oppress us, when, for example, taxes are used to stockpile weapons. Monies are diverted from the weak and greed is rewarded. I need God to liberate me and my compatriots from these unjust attitudes and activities. If we in this country need God's liberation, how much more the voiceless in the underdeveloped countries!

I cry out in prayer; we cry out together in community prayer and are strengthened to take concrete political action against the enemies of justice. We may also have personal enemies who work injustice against us in our neighborhood, our school or shop or firm or hospital or community. We may be physically battered by our husbands, emotionally abused by our wives, or betrayed by our friends. We need to cry out to God with the violence we feel. With this outlet, we need not act violently. With God (sometimes with a therapist) we need to admit our feelings, accept our feelings, welcome them as a share in God's own justice, and then work through these emotions with the Lord. We can do this through the cursing psalms.

Finally, whenever we pray any of the psalms,

formed as community prayer, we pray for the whole
church, our brothers and sisters around the world. Most
of the church lives in the third world, under regimes of
crushing oppression, under the despair which is born of
hunger. Their enemies are viciously real. When we pray,
"May my enemies turn to slime, may all their plans
perish," we need to be identified with these poor, our
sisters and brothers, and to pray out of their hearts.

We know how difficult it is to pray when we are
sick, even attended by nurses in a gleaming hospital
room. Thus we can imagine how difficult it is to pray in
grinding poverty. The sick, the hungry, the frightened in
the crowded huts of the poor can be strengthened by our
prayer. We can imagine how difficult political prisoners
and others who are violated might find it to pray. So, for
them and with them, we call out curses on their oppres-
sors to a listening God.

Historical Psalms

Another type of psalm which might prove difficult
to pray is the historical psalm. We need to understand
two experiences of Jewish spirituality to appreciate the
use of these psalms in our own lives of prayer.

One of the prime tenets of Jewish spirituality is that
remembering makes present. When Israelites of old and
Jews of today remember the experience of the exodus, for
example, that event is present whether four hundred
years later or three thousand years later. Thus when Jews
recount the wonderful works of God on their behalf,
those concrete, historical situations happen again: God is
freeing the oppressed, leading the wandering, raising up
armies, defending cities, giving the harvest, bringing the
exiles back again. When they remember God's acts, God
acts again, today, for them.

A second point to remember in using these often long

and detailed psalms is that as God has chosen and saved and cared for a people with a specific, unique history, so God chooses and saves and cares for our people in our specific history. Our people might be the world or nation or neighborhood or family whom God does free and lead and give to today. "Remember me, Lord, when you save your people," writes the author of Psalm 105.

We can use these historical psalms to recall God's action in our own personal history of salvation. Like the Israelites, God is leading us personally on a journey to freedom, on a pilgrimage not to a promised land, not to heaven, but to God's own self.

Historical psalms call us to remember the Lord's action on our behalf, to praise and thank God for such constant care (*hesed* and *'emet*). To share the fruits of our remembering with a group reveals to them our unique salvation history. Then their thanks for God's work in our life can arise with our own. The remembering of even our personal history invites us to community with others.

Laments, Praise and Thanks

It may be that we were taught never to complain and to hold back tears, to look for the silver lining, to guard against depression, especially any loss of heart so deep that it might border on despair. Yet despair is an emotion, part of being human. The psalmists model these emotions for us as they express their dissatisfaction with the world, themselves, even with God. "Lamah?" they cry. "Why?"

These cries of complaint, these psalms take their name, lament, from the Hebrew word *lamah*, meaning "why?" "My tears are my food day and night" (Ps 42). Why? Why me? Why now? Sometimes the psalmist's grief is spelled out detail by detail.

These psalms encourage us to lay our hearts bare before God, even if they are full of pain, bitterness or despair. Nothing is too insignificant to complain about to a God whose unfailing tenderness we try to trust. We do not sin in despair if we keep on relating to God, not perfectly but just the way we are. God wants to welcome all our feelings.

Finally we note that many psalms are full of praise and thanksgiving, with blessings often depicted in great detail. Even the laments conclude with thanks for God's hearing the pain. One feature of the psalms is their specific attention to God at work both in the nation and in the feelings of the psalmists' own hearts. Every action, every thought, every emotion is referred to the Savior God who creates us good. Praise God! Or, in Hebrew, using a short form of Yahweh, *"Allelu-Ya!"*

Guided Prayer

Psalm 107

> Give thanks to the Lord for God is good; God's love is eternal. Join me in praising the Lord, all you whom God has saved. God has rescued you from your enemies, and brought you back from strange countries.
>
> Some wandered in the trackless desert and could not find a city to live in; they were hungry and thirsty and had given up all hope. In their trouble they called to the Lord, and God saved them from their distress. God led them out, straight to a city to live in. They must thank the Lord for such faithful love, for the wonderful things God did for them. The Lord satisfies those who are hungry and fills them with every good thing.
>
> Some were living in gloom and darkness, prisoners suffering in chains. They were worn out from hard work, falling, with no one to help. In their

trouble they called to the Lord, and God saved them from their distress. God brought them out of darkness and smashed their chains. They must thank the Lord for such faithful love, for the wonders God did for them. The Lord breaks down bronze doors, and smashes iron bars.

Some were sick because of their sins, suffering because of their evil. They couldn't stand the sight of food and were close to dying. In their trouble they called to the Lord, and God saved them from their distress. God healed them with a word and saved them from the grave. They must thank the Lord for such faithful love, for the wonderful things God did for them. They must thank God with sacrifices, and with songs of joy tell all God has done!

Some sailed over the ocean in ships, earning their living on the seas. Their ships were lifted high in the air and plunged down into the depths. In such danger they all lost their courage; they stumbled and staggered like drunks. In their trouble they called to the Lord, and God saved them from all their distress. God stilled the storm and made the waves quiet; God brought them safe to the port they wanted. They must thank the Lord for such faithful love, for the wonderful things God did for them. They must proclaim God's greatness in the assembly of the people.

The Lord has changed deserts into pools of water and dry land into flowing springs. God let hungry people settle there and they built a city to live in. God rescued the needy from their misery, and made their families increase in blessing. May those who are wise think about these things. May they acknowledge the Lord's constant, faithful love.

What God has done for the community of old, God continues to do in our own history of salvation. When in your own life have you been lost, hungry and thirsty? When have you been bound in chains or subdued in spirit? When have you been rebellious, repentant and healed? When have you been carried up to heaven and plunged into the depths? When have you been in deserts and when have you found a home? How have you felt about the Lord during all these times? How do you feel about God as you remember your own history of salvation? Share these feelings with God; that is to pray like the psalmists.

Psalm 23

The Lord is my shepherd. There is nothing I want. In green pastures God leads me and gives me rest. Beside peaceful waters God refreshes me, guiding me in right paths.

Although I walk in a dark valley, I do not fear. For you are at my side with your rod and staff to give me comfort. You spread a banquet before me in the sight of my enemies. You anoint my head with oil and my cup overflows.

Surely goodness and kindness shall follow me all the days of my life. I shall live in the house of the Lord for years to come.

What is your dark valley? What are the things which block your response to life, to people, to God? Ask the Lord to reveal these blocks, whether they be present fears, hostilities, or past hurts. Then repeat slowly: "I fear no evil for you are with me." Bring that verse, that act of trust, with you throughout your day.

Psalm 23

Pray this psalm on a second day. Now focus on all that enhances your response to life, to people, to God.

When has your response to life, your relationships with people and with God been most satisfying? Ask the Lord to reveal these happy or peaceful times to you. Repeat slowly: "Surely goodness and kindness shall follow me all the days of my life." Again, use this verse, this act of trust, throughout the day.

Psalm 103

> Bless the Lord, my innermost heart! All my being, bless God's holy name!
>
> Do not forget all God's kindness, pardoning my sin, healing my diseases. God redeems my life from the grave, blessing me with love and kindness. God fills my life with good things, and renews my youth like an eagle's....
>
> The Lord is merciful and loving, slow to anger, full of steadfast love. God does not keep on scolding us, does not stay angry forever. As high as the heavens are above the earth, so great is God's love for us. As far as the east is from the west, so far does God put our sin away from us. As kind as a father to his children, so kind is God to those who fear.
>
> Our God knows how we are made, God remembers that we are merely dust. Our life is like grass. We grow and flourish like a wild flower. The wind blows and we are gone. No one sees us again.
>
> The Lord's love for those who love endures forever. God's justice lasts forever for those who are faithful to the covenant....

The Hebrew word for blessing means to exchange life. To bless the Lord is to offer God your life. Much of this psalm deals with sin. It is a creaturely, sinful life we offer to God, who knows that we are dust. When we think we are so important and that our sin is the center of the universe, God reminds us that we are dust, and lovable just that way.

God exchanges life, blesses us, in our smallness, our sinfulness. Today, as you pray, offer God the things about yourself that you really don't like. Next time you celebrate Eucharist, that "wondrous exchange," place on the paten your sin and everything in your life which is dusty. God wants you as you are.

From Psalm 115

> To you alone, O Lord, must glory be given, because of your steady love and faithfulness.... The Lord remembers us and blesses us. God blesses the people of Israel....
>
> May you be blessed by the Lord who made heaven and earth.... God is not praised by death, but we the living give thanks, now and forever.

Here it is the Lord who blesses us, who exchanges life with us and with you, intimately. What does it mean for God's life to permeate you? When have you had such an experience? Ask God to bless you again and again during your day. God wants to lavish on you all that God is. Pray to want that too.

From Psalm 116

> What can I offer to God for such great kindness? I will offer a cup of salvation to thank God for saving me.... I am your servant, Lord, and I will serve you just as my family did. You have set me free.
>
> So I will make a sacrifice of thanksgiving, and offer my prayer to you.

Were you to read this psalm in its entirety, you would find every one of the psalmist's pains detailed. All the sorrow, however, alternates with thanks, promises, and prayers. God invites us to remember and share the difficult times; these psalms consecrate our complaints.

Psalm 81

Antiphon: If only we would open our mouths, God would feed us!

Shout with joy to God our savior, sing praise to the God of the universe!

Start the music and play the tambourines, play joyful music on harps and lyres.

Blow the horn for the festival. This is the law, an order from our God.

I heard an unfamiliar voice saying: I took the heavy loads off your backs. I let you put down your workbaskets.

When you were in trouble you called to me and I saved you. From my hiding place in the storm, I answered you.

Listen, my people, to my word. My dear ones, how I wish you would listen to me!

You must never worship an idol or serve anyone but me. I am the Lord, your God.

I brought you out of slavery. Now open your mouth and I will gladly feed you.

How I wish you would listen to me, how I wish you would obey me!

I would quickly defeat all your enemies and your foes. I would feed you with the finest wheat, and with honey I would satisfy you.

Listen to God's longing: How I wish! How much God wants to do for us, if only we would open our mouths, hands and hearts.

Notice what the law is in this psalm. To make music, to sing praise. God wants only our *shalom*, our joy. But we have to be ready, willing, open-hearted to receive.

The Israelites used their bodies in response to God: singing, dancing, clapping in their worship. After praying this psalm a few times, you might try sitting with hands open, turned upward, face turned up, mouth open, asking God to feed you. Sit quietly for as long as you can, waiting for God's fullness.

Exercises

Let the group take five minutes of silence to get in touch with the emotions of the day. Each member then chooses a psalm from the categories below which best describes his/her feeling-tone. Take another five minutes to read/ pray the psalm alone. Then pray aloud and share those parts of the psalm which express your feelings right now.

Praises: 8, 48, 104, 105, 117, 135, 150
Laments: 22, 42, 43, 51, 71, 80
Thanks: 34, 66, 67, 75, 118, 136
Curses: 35, 59, 69, 109, 137, 140

Name one of your favorite psalms and tell why it speaks to you.

Rewrite a psalm in your own words. For example, Psalm 23: "The Lord is my leader; I am not afraid to move on."

On a very down day, compose your own lament and find someone to pray it with you.

For a week pay attention to the media, following a certain situation that you consider unjust. Get inside the skin of the victims of this injustice and write a prayer, even a cursing prayer, out of their skin. Share these modern cursing psalms at your next group meeting.

This will not be a pleasant meeting. You may experience tears and become furious or discouraged. Pray those powerful emotions at the end of the meeting and all the way home. Ask God to channel the energy of your emotion *against* injustice into positive action, however small, for justice here or abroad.

Part Two

6. Jesus

Introduction

"In the fullness of time, God sent a Son..."(Hebrews 1:2). This chapter is the centerpiece of this book. It focuses on the center of human history, the center of our life, God's coming close in the flesh, Jesus.

If you have never studied the leaders, prophets or psalms of Israel, you have known *about* Jesus Christ. I propose that you surely have also known Jesus personally for quite some time.

As adults, it is important to remember and put words to what we already know about a topic. Then, in a biblical fashion, we can put our own past and current experience in dialogue with the community tradition.

In this case, I will first draw out your experience of Jesus, asking you to share it verbally, preferably in a faith-sharing group, but at least with one other believer.

Thus you will experience the very methodology by which Scripture was formed: friends of God experienced God/Jesus/Spirit, reflected on their experience, shared it in community, and eventually wrote it down. Later communities of believers "canonized" these religious experiences, agreeing to include certain writings in the canon of Scripture.

When we pray with Scripture, we take up the record of these religious experiences. Like Mary, we "ponder all these things" in our hearts. Through the Spirit who breathes life into these biblical words, we hope to experience God/Jesus/Spirit with our ancestors in the faith. We want to experience as really present with and active in our lives the God who came so close to Moses and Peter, Mary and Paul.

So, in this chapter, I will change my methodology and begin with exercises, preferably worked in a group. Then I will comment, and finally, offer suggestions for prayer.

Exercises

In the Gospel, Jesus asked, "Who do people say that I am?" Those words are addressed to us too. Share what people today believe about Jesus. Limit the time of your discussion.

Then get personal. "Who do *you* say that I am?" Take five minutes for silent reflection. In a faith sharing style (no discussion, no judgments) tell the group who Jesus is for you personally.

Gospels are not historical documents, nor do they offer a biography of Jesus. They are proclamations of the good news about Jesus. Each evangelist and his community remembered different things about Jesus because their memories of him were affected by their own lives. The resurrection of Jesus, his passion, certain incidents from his life, and certain of his words helped people make sense of their own joys and pains, victories and failures.

Without copying from any of the four Gospels, or even rereading favorite sections, simply remember the gospel stories and teachings. Then spend half an hour writing your own gospel. What about all that Jesus did and said is important in your life? That is good news (gospel) for you. Share your gospel with your group. Your family might appreciate hearing it too.

Read the passion account in Mark 15. Read John 19. Were there or were there not women at the foot of the cross? Did Jesus cry out, abandoned by God, or was he composed, full of dignity? Discuss. Which portrayal of Jesus speaks more to you? Why? Share that.

Remember that there is no right or wrong. Both accounts are included in the scriptural canon to help us know Jesus in his dying and to help us in our own pain, loss and preparation for dying.

Read Luke 24 and John 20-21. What similarities between these two accounts of the resurrection can your group find? What differences? Speculate: Why might there be so many differences?

Listen to "St. Matthew's Passion" by Johann Sebastian Bach. Share what thoughts and feelings arise in you.

If God was understood by Jewish authors of Scripture as so passionate, how would you expect to find Jesus, the ultimate expression of God? In your group name all the deeply-felt emotions of Jesus that you can remember.

An ancient doctrine of the Church is: "Whatever is not assumed by Christ is not redeemed." The author of Hebrews said it earlier: "Jesus is like us in everything but sin." Sin, to the author of Hebrews, would not mean "missing the mark," a Jewish description of ordinary sin. Nor would it mean the Jewish equivalent of mortal sin, uncleanness; Jesus deliberately did unclean things, showing us that God's thoughts (about sin) are not necessarily our thoughts. Rebellion, or "sinning with a high hand," is the sin meant by the author of Hebrews when he writes that Jesus is like us in everything but sin (Hebrews 2:17-18; 4:15).

Jesus as completely human would have felt every human passion. Feelings, even such emotions as lust, greed, jealousy, and hatred, are not sinful. They are human. Emotions need to be felt and acknowledged so that their power over us can be broken by a liberator God who yearns to set us free.

If we were ever taught that simply feeling our feelings was sin, let us look again at Jesus, "tempted as we are, but without sin" (Hebrews 4:15). When a feeling arises it signals to us that we are in danger (fear, anger), that we have suffered loss (grief), or that we have what we want (love). Other emotions play on these four basic themes: love, fear, anger, grief. There is a range of each emotion; for example, anger may range from annoyance to rage to hatred. We feel. Then we are meant to decide how to act. Only in the deciding/acting lies sin.

To decide we first need truthful information. Am I sensing and thinking correctly? Yes, that is a semi-trailer bearing down on my rear bumper. Fear pumps energy into my bloodstream. The emotion triggers not only sweat but a stomping on my gas pedal, a heightened awareness of the lane next to me, a split second decision to flick on my turn signal, and to MOVE.

Another example, one Jesus warned about: lusting in our hearts. We may have been wrongly taught that sexual feeling is automatically a sin. Let us imagine that a stranger walks by on the beach. I am in awe at the beautiful body, I have an involuntary rush of emotion and longing. In other words, the stimulus has triggered sexual arousal. That is not sin, that is human.

Jesus, truly human, would of course have been sexually aroused. But he did not lust in his heart. He would have felt the emotion, perhaps would have thanked God for both his feeling and the beauty of the person and then let it go. He would have decided not to act. Even in his mind he would not have treated this person as an object.

In your group list all kinds of emotions that human beings experience. Then, using your imaginations and the insights of the Spirit, imagine when Jesus might have experienced each of those emotions—when he might have: fallen in love or felt greedy, guilty, possessive, scared, sad, confused, and so forth. Discuss. Try to stay open to even "wild" images of Jesus' feelings. The Spirit, Jesus promised, will guide the community "in all truth" (John 16:13). Remember that the Spirit is with you, trying to teach you how very real the humanity of Jesus is.

Gospels have been described as passion accounts with extended introductions. We tend to think of Jesus' suffering as concentrated in his last fifteen to twenty hours. Take five minutes to remember gospel stories in which Jesus suffered at other times in his life. Share your memories of him.

The word "passion" may also be understood as desire (as, for example, she has a passion for tennis). What did Jesus passionately desire? What did God passionately desire for Jesus?

Some people are afraid to get close to God. They say, "Look what God did to Jesus." They remember, of course, the agony in the garden, when Jesus prayed, "Not my will but yours be done" (Mark 14:36). Then the soldiers hauled him off to violence and death. What did God passionately desire for Jesus in the garden? What does God passionately desire for you? Stop and reflect.

Sometimes we try to console someone in grief by saying:

"This must be God's will." The God whom Jesus knows and teaches does not passionately desire anyone's suffering. On the contrary, God passionately hates human suffering. No wonder that when Jesus, put flesh on God's *hesed* and *'emet*, he exhausted himself healing physical pain and the suffering of being outcast. Jesus hated death and groaned in agony over the death of his friend Lazarus. Jesus was mirroring God's desire to heal us. "My plans for you are plans of peace, wholeness, *shalom*" (Jeremiah 29:11).

How would you comfort someone in grief? In your group role-play various responses. Try to come to a consensus about the most Christ-like comfort you can offer another in times of suffering.

Through these exercises I hope you have discovered your lively love and admiration for Jesus. You probably also discovered that your beliefs about him vary. Varied understandings of Jesus course through the pages of the New Testament. In other words, we discover many Christologies, or understandings of Christ, in the early Church. We can discover many Christologies in today's Church if we honestly speak to each other and dare to say who Christ is. Because Jesus, like God and like us, is a mystery, he is infinitely knowable. Who do you say he is, now that you've listened to your group? There are no right or wrong answers, just the multifaceted wonder of the mystery: Jesus Christ.

New Testament Christologies

In the first communities of Christians some thought that Jesus was a prophet, others a wonder-worker. Some thought he would become Messiah (the anointed one, the Christ) at the end of the world, others thought he was made Christ at his resurrection. Mark thinks Jesus became

Son of God at his baptism by John; Matthew and Luke believe he was Son of God from the time of his birth; John explains that the uniquely begotten Word of God pre-existed all creation. It took centuries of debate, philosophizing and even war before the Council of Chalcedon in 451 promulgated a "definition" of Jesus Christ. That Council used philosophical ideas and language which today confuse rather than clarify. We stand on surer ground if we describe Jesus rather than try to define him, as we contemplate the mystery of the incarnation.

The authors of the New Testament did not presume to define; they did not offer a systematic Christology. In John's Gospel, for example, the evangelist contradicts himself about Jesus' relationship with the Father: "The Father and I are one"; "The Father is greater than I." In Paul's letters we find various Christologies as well. What the evangelists did, so beautifully, was to tell the story of Jesus in such a way that our own personal stories and the stories of our communities could be enriched and given meaning by his. Through reading the Gospels, we are meant to participate in the experiences of Jesus. In John 20:31, the evangelist explains that he has written so that we might have faith that Jesus is the Christ. He hopes that through faith (knowing Jesus, trusting and clinging to him) we may have life.

Therefore, we approach the Gospels to know Jesus, the historical man. We also come to know Christ, the risen Lord always present in his communities, wherever two or three are gathered in his name. We attend to the truth and reality of his person, not "truths" about him. Instead of forcing a unity of detail on the four Gospels, trying to harmonize them, we can learn to live with the ambiguities.

We want to reach beneath the facts of a gospel story to be engaged by the meaning of the story. For example, why does only Luke portray Jesus' crib as a manger, whereas Matthew situates the holy family in a house in

Bethlehem? Harmonizers would try to explain the discrepancy by assuring us that after a few weeks there was room in the inn for the newborn and his parents. There is no need to manipulate the Gospels like this.

We need, instead, to ask Luke's meaning in writing the truth of Jesus' first home as Luke and his community see it. This truth may not correspond to historical fact; the family may indeed have had a house in Bethlehem. Yet for Luke and his community, who understood history differently than we do in an age of instant retrieval of fact, it is important that Jesus' identification with the poor and outcast begins even at his birth. Luke symbolizes that identification by having Mary lay the homeless infant in a manger. That Jesus understands the pain of the poor and wants to share their suffering even from infancy is good news, Gospel, for the poor and outcast. Jesus is attractive to them because of this almost insignificant image in Luke's Gospel. If any of this disturbs you, I strongly recommend *Who Do You Say That I Am*, by Rev. Edward Ciuba (Alba House), and *The Words of Jesus in Our Gospel* by Stanley Marrow, S.J. (Paulist).

Jesus Reveals Himself Uniquely

We briefly sketched the various Christologies in the New Testament to illustrate that faith in Jesus is unique to each of us because Jesus reveals himself to us personally, uniquely. Of course he reveals himself to communities, as he did to the earliest communities, as he did at the Council of Chalcedon, through the working of his Spirit. We, like the bishops and grass-roots Christians of those first four centuries, need to discover Jesus in the gospel of our own lives and to share our discoveries with each other, building community truth.

There is such richness if we dare to express in a group who Jesus is for us personally. No one's description is perfect, nor is it wrong. Faith is a gift and each of us receives a unique share in knowledge about Jesus. Jesus is the giver of faith, revealing himself uniquely to this person in this way at this time.

I have heard parents despair over their teenager's lack of faith. For example, "My son likes Jesus, thinks he's a cool teacher, great pacifist. I try to explain that he is God, and my boy just gives me an exasperated shrug and walks away. If he'd listen I could prove that Jesus is God by using the miracles." So many of us were taught to prove the resurrection, to prove Christ's divinity. However, mysteries of faith like all that is implied in the resurrection, or Christ's divinity, cannot be proved. We can demonstrate and describe and surely use our minds as well as our hearts to plumb the depths of these mysteries. Yet anything that can be proved no longer requires faith. In faith, God's gift of faith, we trust and know at a deep intuitive and personal level that Jesus is risen, alive, divine.

Once we may have become fascinated by our logic, by the reasonableness of a faith that became more and more a deposit of truths which we could hurl at scoffers. Now our own adult children have become the scoffers. Pope John XXIII understood the exasperated shrugs of a bored world and so he called a Council. He urged the bishops to find new interpretations for ancient doctrines, to find new and meaningful language to express our faith.

Incarnation as Process

One of our chief doctrines is the mystery of the incarnation. In pre-Vatican II days we would have been warned away from mysteries as impossible to understand. Why engage in exercises of futility? Catholic theologian Karl Rahner writes that mystery is that which is infinitely knowable, and so challenges us to question and search, think and pray.

This approach to the incarnation, using today's philosophy and language instead of that of the fifth century, might be helpful. Certainly we are all more aware of process. Process is as important as product. Growth is a process, not to be hurried. Let us suppose, then, that the incarnation, the Word of God's taking flesh, was a process. Once we may have pinpointed the incarnation as a moment of time in Mary's womb. Suppose, however, that the Word of God was ever more and more completely taking flesh, day by day becoming human. We all are in a process of becoming more and more truly human. Why not God's Son? Jesus grew "in wisdom and age and grace," Luke writes, and then he repeats it (Luke 2:40, 52).

To grow in wisdom is to become more fully human, and sharing in God's wisdom is to become more fully divine. To grow in grace is to grow in the life and likeness of God. Humans have more capacity for wisdom and grace at seventeen than at seven. So would Jesus love more humanly and more divinely at thirty than when he was ten. To give God glory, Jesus would have grown more fully human, more completely alive. His most total moment of aliveness, paradoxically, was the moment of his dying. Then truly "the glory of God is the human being, fully human, fully alive" (St. Irenaeus).

We and our children are also in process of growing in wisdom and grace, receiving the gift of faith, receiving Jesus' revelation of who he is. We are all at various points in that process. Some of us might quite honestly give intellectual assent to a set of divinely revealed truths; others quite honestly cannot. We will not be saved, however, because of intellectual assent. We will be saved by that faith in Jesus which means relationship with him: knowing him, opening to him, trusting him, responding to him, learning from him, walking with him. Only Jesus saves; our faith is our wholehearted response.

This chapter is the centerpiece of our journey. God has come close, closer than we could dare to imagine, in this simple carpenter called to comfort and challenge, to preach and embody the good news of God's constant care. We are invited "to hear, to see with our own eyes, to look on, to touch with our own hands" the word of life made visible (1 John 1:1-2), made flesh.

As we move directly then into the New Testament we want to "keep our eyes fixed on Jesus, the pioneer and perfecter of our faith" (Hebrews 12:2). Our purpose is to know Jesus directly. We ask for open hearts so that our "searching the Scriptures" will not be merely theoretical. Jesus cries out against the Pharisees:

"You study the Scriptures believing that in them you have eternal life.

These Scriptures witness to me, yet you refuse to come to me for life" (John 5:39-40).

We study the Scriptures only to come to Jesus for life. Jewish rabbis taught that to study Scripture is to worship. May our experience be one of worship as we keep our eyes fixed on Jesus and study the Scriptures.

Guided Prayer

The Gospels are called "passion accounts with extended introductions." Of all that we could focus on in the events of Jesus' life, death and resurrection, we will highlight the passion of Jesus. The following passages carry two meanings of passion: 1) strong, deep, long-lasting emotion; 2) suffering which permeated Jesus' whole life, as it does our own.

Remember that even to read Scripture is to pray. Prayer is a dialogue, and God speaks to us in the Word.

Whatever we think, whatever we feel, whatever desires or images arise in us, whatever way we respond to the Word is our part of the dialogue, is prayer.

John 11:38-44

> At the death of his friend, Lazarus, Jesus was deeply disturbed. He came to the tomb, a cave, with a stone across it. Jesus said, "Take away that stone."
>
> Martha, sister of the dead man, said, "Lord, by now he will smell; he has been dead for four days."
>
> Jesus said to her, "Did I not say that if you believe you will see the glory of God?" So they took away the stone. Then Jesus lifted his eyes and said, "Father, I thank you for hearing me. I know you always hear me, but I have said this because of the people here, that they may believe that you have sent me." Then he cried, "Lazarus, come out!"
>
> The dead man came out, bound hand and foot with burial cloths; even his face was bound with cloth. So Jesus said to them, "Untie him and let him go free."

Jesus stands in pain, in tears before the tomb and calls out for new life. Lazarus, come forth. Both men are fully alive. Imagine their meeting.

What parts of your own life are dead? Hear Jesus cry your name: _____, come forth! _____ live! Respond to his call.

Let him/her go free. Jesus speaks those words to you and to your friends. Where are you tied up? Whom can you allow close enough to help untie you? Who has helped you be free in the past?

In what do you find life, joy? Your aliveness is a gift. With whom is Jesus asking you to share your life now?

Luke 19:41-44; 12:49-53; Hebrews 5:7

As Jesus drew near to Jerusalem, he saw the city and began to weep. He cried, "If only you knew how to find peace today—but it is hidden from you. Days are coming when your enemies will hem you in on all sides, smash you to the ground, destroy your children and not leave one stone upon another. You never understood that this was your time of visitation."

Jesus cried out, "I have come to bring fire to the earth. How I wish it were already blazing! There is a baptism into which I must be plunged. How deep is my anguish until it is accomplished! Do you think I come to bring peace to the earth? No! I come to bring division. From now on households and families will be divided...."

In the days when he was in the flesh, Jesus offered prayers and petitions with loud cries and tears to the one who was able to save him from death. He was heard because of his reverence.

"Loud cries" in Hebrews 5:7 means, in Greek, the screams of a wild animal which is trapped. This is the author's understanding of Jesus' agony in the garden, his panic. What do you feel when listening to Jesus express his deep desires, fears, frustrations, anger? Here is a passionate man. From where does this intensity come? How do you feel about human passion, about intense people? Where does your passion lie? Talk with Jesus about these aspects of being an alive human being.

Mark 3:20-21; 6:1-5

Jesus came to his home in Capernaum. Again a crowd gathered, making it impossible for Jesus and his disciples to eat. When his family heard about this they set out from Nazareth to take charge of him, for people were saying he was out of his mind....

His mother and his brothers arrived. Standing outside they sent word into him. The crowd told him, "Your mother and brothers and sisters are outside asking for you." Looking around at those seated in the circle, he replied, "Here are my mother and my brothers. Whoever does the will of God is my brother and sister and mother."

He came to his hometown, accompanied by his disciples. On the sabbath, he began to teach in the synagogue, and many who heard him were amazed. They asked, "Where did this man get all this? What kind of wisdom is this? What mighty deeds he can do! Isn't he the carpenter, son of Mary, brother of James, Joses, Judas and Simon? Aren't his sisters here with us?" They took offense at him.

Can you identify with Jesus, feel like him, feel rejected, perhaps even by your family (only if at some time in your life you felt rejected)? Can you speak with him about rejection, asking him to talk to you about how he felt? How do you feel toward him as you listen? Speak with him about the incident in your life. How does he feel as he listens to your hurt?

Mark 5:22-24, 35-40

A synagogue official named Jairus fell at Jesus' feet and pleaded urgently with him, "My daughter is dying. Please come and lay your hands on her that she may be healed and live." So Jesus went off with him....

While Jesus was still speaking, people from Jairus' house arrived and said, "Your daughter has died. Why bother the master further?" Jesus paid no attention but said to Jairus, "Do not be afraid. Have faith...." When they arrived at the house, Jesus saw the commotion, people weeping and wailing loudly. He went in and said to them, "Why this uproar and weeping? The child is not dead, only asleep." And they laughed him to scorn....

Has anyone ever mocked or ridiculed you? Identify with Jesus, trying to get deep into his feelings. You are trying to help and everyone laughs at you. Tell your Father how you feel. Ask God for what you need. Try to hear-see-sense your Father's response to you.

Matthew 8:19-20

A scribe approached Jesus and said to him, "Master, I will follow you wherever you go." Jesus said to him, "Foxes have dens, birds of the sky have nests, but the Son of Man has nowhere to rest his head."

One of the great sufferings these days in Church and society is constant change and insecurity. Jesus can call no place home; he has no earthly security, has no idea who will care for him in his old age, does not know how long the crowds and the disciples will be with him before they tire of his non-political message. Try to be with Jesus to let him share the insecurities of his life. Then speak with him about your insecurities.

John 6:59-68

He said these things (about eating his flesh and drinking his blood) while teaching in the synagogue in Capernaum. Then many of his disciples who had been listening said, "This saying is difficult. Who could accept it?"

Jesus knew his disciples were murmuring about this, so he said to them, "Does this shock you? What if you saw the Son of Man ascending to where he was before? I tell you, it is the spirit which gives life; the flesh counts for nothing here. These words I have spoken are spirit and life. But there are some here who do not believe.... For this reason I told you that no one can come to me unless my Father draw that person."

At that many of his disciples left him, returning to their former way of life, for they could no longer accompany him. Jesus then turned to the twelve. "Do you want to leave too?" he asked. Simon Peter replied, "Master to whom could we go? You have the words of eternal life."

Perhaps one of Jesus' deepest sufferings is expressed in his question: "Will you also go away?" What hurts more than the fear of rejection and abandonment by the very people we thought were friends? He is not play-acting with that question, not testing the twelve. He is really afraid of being deserted by his friends. He expresses his feelings of fear, anxiety. Can you feel what he is feeling? Have you ever felt left out, left behind? Have you ever felt as though your companions would walk away from you disgusted if they ever found out what you were like deep inside? Speak with Jesus about these feelings that you both share.

Hebrews 12:1-2

Surrounded by all these witnesses to the faith, let us throw off everything that weighs us down, every sin to which we cling, and run with determination the race in which we are entered. Let us keep our eyes fixed on Jesus, the pioneer and perfecter of our faith, who endured the cross, making light of its shame for the sake of the joy which lay ahead of him, sitting at the right hand of God.

Jesus is our pioneer, going before us, opening a new way to God through himself, his body.

Remember three or four incidents in the past year that brought you pain. Did Jesus ever go through something similar to your situation? Remember some incidents of joy. Did Jesus ever experience situations like yours? Hebrews tells that he is like us in everything but rebellion. How is Jesus like you? How do you feel about his sharing humanity with you, sharing weakness and strength?

Contemplation is, simply, looking at Jesus, trying to be with him in his life, trying to feel his feelings. It is a way of letting him share his mind and his heart with us so that when we relate to the body of Christ today we may think his thoughts and love with his love. Some days his words like "Will you also go away?" may evoke such strong remembrance of our own pain that we have to speak with Jesus about it. Other days we may be drawn to stay with Jesus' feelings rather than our own. Both are excellent ways to pray Scripture, to let God come very close.

7. God's Compassion Come Close: Luke's Gospel

Poet Robert Frost once remarked that teachers don't teach material; rather, a good teacher teaches himself or herself. From the twenty-seven books of the New Testament, I have selected just a few for our focus, five which continually nourish and challenge me. I will, in a way, be teaching myself, just as our four evangelists had to select from among many stories and sayings of Jesus and thus teach their unique viewpoint, theology, spirituality.

I begin with Luke's Gospel because of its author's point of view. When one lays this Gospel alongside of Matthew's and Mark's, much of the material is the same. It is, however, Luke's differences from the other two which highlight what was of greatest concern to him and his community. With the rest of the scholarly community, I maintain that Luke the evangelist was neither companion of Paul, nor confidant of Mary, nor a physician. I believe he was Jewish, but trained by Greeks both in secular subjects and in Scripture. His narrative style is excellent and his biblical spirituality is deep. He portrays Jesus as God's compassion in the flesh.

Jesus' Prophetic Spirit and Word

As with each Gospel, Jesus is the centerpiece. Luke envisions Jesus as a prophet, filled with the Spirit to challenge the rich and powerful but particularly to comfort the poor and outcast. The word of God which Jesus preaches is addressed universally to all kinds of people, to all the nations.

Even before Jesus' birth, the Spirit moves powerfully in the lives of Zechariah, Elizabeth and Mary. Their inspired speech and songs are gifts of the Spirit. With the Spirit's power hovering over her, Mary's unique gift from the Spirit is her Son. The same Spirit drives the man Jesus through his ministry. "Jesus, armed with the power of the Spirit, returned to Galilee," came to the synagogue at Nazareth, and, having opened the scroll of Isaiah, proclaimed the beginning of his prophetic service (Luke 4:14-20). The Spirit will continue Jesus' mission and ministry through the empowering of "the Eleven and the rest of the company." They wait for the Spirit-promise of God (Luke 24). Indeed, the second volume of Luke's work, Acts of the Apostles, is a kind of Gospel of the Holy Spirit.

Like every prophetic word, the word of God that Jesus wields, critiques the rich and powerful of this world. John the Baptizer issues a call for social justice (3:10-16), which Jesus continues. His "woe to you" statements warn the self-satisfied (6:24-26). Simon, his host at a banquet, is unfavorably compared with a disreputable woman (7:36-50). Rich fools, described in 12:13-21, are headed for destruction. Jesus offers a parable of such a rich, stingy man who ignores the begging Lazarus (6:19-31) and strikes again at religious "riches" in the parable of the Pharisee and the publican who came to pray (18:10-14).

Through Jesus' prophetic word, God comforts the poor. To be in solidarity with the poor, Jesus would have to know and share their poverty. Luke describes the birth of Jesus in just that way. In Bethlehem, far from "home," his parents have to journey through territory infested with bandits, find a manger for the child, welcome the poor and outcast shepherds. In the temple his parents make the offering of the poor (2:24). "Blessed are you poor," the adult Jesus addresses the crowds (not like Matthew's "Blessed are the poor in spirit").

The good news to the poor is that God, like a father, loves them and comes running down the road to meet them. God welcomes them home and feasts them and their friends, according to the parable of the prodigal son, which might better be titled the story of the prodigal or extravagant father (Luke 15:11-32).

Jesus with Outcasts

Closely linked with the poor in Luke's theology are sinners and outcasts from society. Only Luke carries stories about foreigners who find favor with God, stories in which Jesus praises the widow of Sarepta and Naaman the Syrian (4:25-30). Only Luke hands on two stories of the outcast Samaritans. One is a compassionate man who helps a victim of violence (10:29-37); the other is a leper, grateful for Jesus' healing (17:11-19). Tax collectors like Zacchaeus (19:1-10) and the thieves crucified with him (23:39-43) are offered reconciliation; both are incidents unique to Luke's Gospel.

Finally, a major class of Jewish outcasts were women. To most husbands, and certainly in the eyes of the teachers of the law, they were property, only a bit more valuable than cattle. Yet in Luke's Gospel they receive a prominent role in Jesus' infancy: Mary, Elizabeth, Anna. To indicate Mary's importance, Luke has Mary receive the angel's message. In Matthew's more Jewish Gospel Mary is kept in the dark while Joseph is told the child's origins and name.

When Luke names a man, a woman is often paired with him: for example, Simeon/Anna; widow of Sarepta/Naaman the Syrian. When a situation appealing to a man is used in Jesus' teaching, the next example often appeals to a woman: shepherd searching for a sheep/woman searching for a coin (15:1-10); God's reign is like a grain of mustard seed which a man sowed/like leaven which a woman hid in meal (13:18-20). Jonah is a sign/queen of the south is a sign (11:29-32). Women accompany Jesus as disciples (8:1-3); they entertain him and learn from him as Martha and Mary did (10:38-42). Luke alone hands on the episode of the women weeping as Jesus carries his cross to Calvary (23:27-32).

Three women are carefully depicted with great tenderness by Luke. The first is the nameless woman of ill repute (wrongly identified with Mary of Magdala) who weeps so unabashedly that she washes Jesus' feet with her tears and kisses them. Her great love in action becomes a touchstone for a major message of Jesus in Luke's Gospel: "Her sins are forgiven because she has loved much" (7:36-50).

The second woman is also noted only by Luke. A woman was attending synagogue while Jesus was teaching, a woman bent over for eighteen years. "She could not fully straighten herself." Jesus calls to her and announces her freedom from her handicap. When the president of the synagogue scolds, not Jesus, but the people for coming to be healed on the Sabbath, Jesus responds harshly. Religious leaders, he charges, wouldn't hesitate to care for their oxen or asses on the Sabbath, so why not care for "this woman, a daughter of Abraham?" The woman stands straight and the people rejoice (13:10-17).

The third woman is Mary, the mother of Jesus. The evangelist Mark quickly dismisses Mary after she tries to take Jesus home, sure that he is out of his mind (Mark 3:21, 31). Matthew allows her a role, but quite subordinate to Joseph's, in the infancy narratives, his only mention of her. John places her in two key positions: at Cana and at the cross. Luke, however, focuses on her relatives and her activities in the infancy stories and accords her a major hymn, the Magnificat.

In a cryptic passage (11:27-28) it seems that Jesus puts down Mary. A woman in the crowd calls out to Jesus: "Blessed is the womb which bore you and the breasts you sucked." Jesus replies: "Blessed rather are those who hear the word of God and keep it." Luke has set the stage for this little drama in his first chapter when Mary responds, "Be it done to me according to your word" (1:38). Mary is not to be praised for physical motherhood.

If anyone "kept" the word of God, it certainly was Mary, whom Luke portrays as keeping and pondering the word (2:19, 51). Jesus again raises women's dignity in an anti-feminine society, saying in fact that women have every right to be hearers of the word, that is, disciples. Luke has named Mary the first disciple, a model disciple, one who is taught by God in the depths of her heart.

One final unique contribution of Luke to our own spiritual development: while in Matthew Jesus' disciples are commissioned by the risen Lord to teach and baptize, in Luke they are sent to offer an opportunity for reconciliation. "Repentance and forgiveness of sins should be preached in his name to all nations" (24:47). Luke's entire Gospel could be called good news of reconciliation and forgiveness, a Gospel in which Jesus feels a gut level response of compassion for the sinful, the weak, and the alienated (literally, his bowels are moved with compassion).

Jesus embodies God's own compassion. In a significant change from Matthew's Gospel, Luke does not ask us to be perfect as our heavenly Father is perfect but, instead, to be compassionate as our heavenly Father is compassionate (6:34-36). When I ask people all over the country to finish the verse, "Be you _____ as your heavenly Father is _____," a unanimous chorus of "perfect" resounds. Perhaps only five percent have ever even heard of Luke's version, "Be you compassionate as your heavenly Father is compassionate." Yet many of the people I meet in class, counseling or spiritual direction tell me their goal in life is "to love well." How encouraging, then, is Luke's message to love well, to grow in compassion. The Jesus of Luke's Gospel not only urges us but models so well a Spirit-filled life of attention to and care for God's poor and those crushed in spirit. Jesus commissions us, too, to offer compassion, forgiveness, and reconciliation to all peoples.

Luke's Gospel currently is receiving attention from scholars and laity alike. As the Church community becomes more imbued with a call and commitment to social justice, Jesus in Luke's Gospel offers a model for attending to the needs of the poor and the outcast. A renewal of the Spirit's outpouring is the felt experience of many Christians in our day. "Jesus, driven by the power of the Spirit" (Luke 4:14), comes in our time to preach a word of comfort to the downtrodden, a word of challenge to the comfortable through our own prophetic mission and ministry as Church. The Spirit impels us, as disciples of Jesus, to a universal compassion, to a global reconciliation. We ourselves are comforted and challenged in those tasks as we read and pray with Luke's Gospel.

Guided Prayer

Luke 1:26-38

      The angel Gabriel was sent from God to Mary, a young woman in a town in Galilee called Nazareth.

She was engaged to be married to a man from the house of David, Joseph. The angel greeted her: "Hail, full of grace. The Lord is with you."

She was greatly disturbed at this and pondered what sort of greeting this might be.

Then the angel said to her, "Do not be afraid, Mary, for you have found favor with God. Look, you are going to conceive and have a son. You shall give him the name Jesus. He will be great, and will be called the Son of the Most High. The Lord God will give him the throne of king David, his ancestor. He will rule over the house of Jacob forever, and his reign will never end."

Mary said, "How can this be? I have never been that close with a man."

The angel replied, "The Holy Spirit will come upon you. The power of the Most High will overshadow you. Therefore the child to be born will be holy, Son of God.... Nothing is impossible with God."

Mary replied, "Yes, I am the servant of the Lord. Let it be done to me just as you say."

Where did the message from the Lord come to Mary? Was she cooking, working in the fields, drawing water? Where does the Lord's message come to you? She is confused and fearful. What messages from God have confused and frightened you? Talk them over with God.

"The Holy Spirit will overshadow you." In Genesis the Spirit overshadows the waters of chaos and brings life from whatever seems empty. Ask the Spirit to bring life and peace to whatever seems void, chaotic in your life.

Luke 7:36-50

A Pharisee invited Jesus to dinner, so he came and reclined at table. There was a sinful woman in town who discovered he was eating at the Pharisee's. So she brought in an alabaster jar of ointment. She stood at Jesus' feet and began to cry. Her tears washed over his feet. She then wiped his feet with her hair and kissed them. Finally, she anointed them with the special oil.

When the host saw all this he said to himself: if Jesus were truly a prophet he would know what sort of woman this is who is touching him. She is a sinner. Jesus spoke up: "Simon, I have something to say to you." "What is it, Master?" he asked. Jesus said, "Two people owed money to the same person. One owed 500 days' wages and the other owed 50 days' wages. Neither one was able to repay the debt, so the creditor wrote off both their debts. Who will love that creditor more?"

Simon answered, "The one with the larger debt, I suppose."

To Simon, Jesus said, "Right." Then he turned to the woman, but continued to speak to Simon, "Look at this woman. When I entered your house you did not give me water to wash my feet, but she has bathed them with her tears, wiping them with her hair. You did not greet me with the customary kiss, but she has not stopped kissing my feet since I came in. You did not anoint my head with oil, but she anointed my feet with ointment. So I tell you, Simon, her many sins are forgiven. She has shown great love. The one who is forgiven little loves little." Then he said to the woman, "Your sins are forgiven.... Your faith has saved you. Go in peace."

Our relationship with Jesus often swings between centering on our needs (prayer) and looking at him with love (contemplation). This woman asks for nothing; she

simply expresses her admiration and love. Look at Jesus
looking at her with admiration and love. Now Jesus looks
directly at you. How do you respond?

Luke 4:1-13

> Filled with the Holy Spirit, Jesus came up from
> the Jordan and was led into the wilderness by the
> Spirit. For forty days he was tempted by the devil.
> After eating nothing for all those days, at the end he
> was hungry.
>
> The devil then said to him, "If you are the Son of
> God, command this stone to become bread." Jesus
> replied, "It is in the scripture: one does not live on
> bread alone."
>
> Then the devil took him to a high spot and
> showed him the kingdoms of the world in a single
> moment, saying to Jesus: "I will give you the power
> and glory of all this, for it has been handed to me to
> give to whom I wish. All this will be yours if you
> just worship me."
>
> Jesus replied, "It is written in scripture: You
> shall worship the Lord your God. God alone shall
> you serve."
>
> Then the devil led him to Jerusalem to stand on
> the parapet of the temple, saying: "If you are the
> Son of God, throw yourself down, for it is written:
> God will command the angels to guard you, and
> they will hold you up, lest you dash your foot
> against a stone." Jesus replied, "It is also written:
> You shall not put the Lord, your God, to the test."
> When the devil had finished every temptation, he
> left Jesus for a while.

Identify with Jesus being led by the Spirit into the
desert. Use your imagination and feelings to get more
totally involved in this living word/event. Feel the hot

wind, the sand, the hunger. Tell the Holy Spirit how you feel interiorly. Comfort Jesus in his hunger, his temptation. What will you do? say?

Luke 4:14-21

> Jesus returned to Galilee in the power of the Spirit. News about him spread throughout the region and when he taught in their synagogues he was praised by everyone. He came to Nazareth where he had grown up. As usual he went to synagogue on the Sabbath. He stood up to read and was handed the scroll of the prophet Isaiah. So he unrolled the scroll and found the passage where it was written:
>
> The Spirit of the Lord is upon me, because God has anointed me and sent me to announce good news to the poor. To proclaim freedom to the captives and recovery of sight to the blind. To heal the broken hearted and to proclaim the year of God's favor.
>
> Rolling up the scroll, he handed it back to the attendant and sat down. The eyes of everyone in the synagogue were on him intensely. He then said to them: "Today this passage of scripture has come to fruition. You have heard it."

Keep your eyes intensely on Jesus. Now read this passage out loud, but in your imagination watch him, his movements, gestures, facial expression. Hear the tone and volume of his voice. This is contemplation, according to St. Ignatius Loyola. Sit in the synagogue and be with him. Pay attention to him. Contemplation is that simple.

Luke 22:42-44

> After supper Jesus went out to the Mount of Olives. After withdrawing about a stone's throw

from his friends, he knelt and prayed, "Father, if you are willing, take this cup away from me. Yet, not my will but yours be done...." In anguish, he prayed even more urgently. His sweat fell to the ground like clots of blood.

Look at Jesus, feel with Jesus in this experience of anxiety before his suffering. Try to use as many of your senses as you can. Hear the trees in the garden rustling, feel the wind, smell the fresh crispness of the night.

In feeling with him, let your own anxieties surface. What worries you, of what are you afraid, what do you dread? Let your stomach knot up, your head throb if need be. Share your emotions with Jesus. Then try to listen as he talks about his fears. Try to comfort him, to understand him (which is comfort). Remember that contemplation is, simply, looking at Jesus, trying to be with him in his life, trying to feel his feelings. In prayer we let him share his mind and his heart with us so that when we relate to the body of Christ, the Church-community of today, we may think his thoughts and love with his love.

Luke 24:35-53

The two returned and told what had happened on their way to Emmaus, how the Lord revealed himself in the breaking of the bread. While they were still talking about this, Jesus stood in the midst of them, saying, "Peace be with you."

They were startled, terrified. They thought they were seeing a ghost. Jesus said to them, "Why are you troubled? Why do doubts arise in your hearts? Look at my hand and my feet. It is I. Touch me and see. A ghost does not have flesh and bones as you can see I do." As he was saying this, he showed them his hands and his feet. They still could not believe because of joy. They were thoroughly amazed. So he asked them, "Do you have anything here to eat?" They handed him a piece of baked fish. He took it and ate it in front of them.

Then he said, "Remember my words which I spoke to you while I was still with you, how everything about me in the law of Moses, everything written in the prophets, must come to fruition." With that, he opened their minds to understand the Scriptures.

He continued, "It is written that the anointed one would suffer and rise from the dead on the third day. It is written that repentance for forgiveness of sins would be preached in the Messiah's name to all the nations, beginning in Jerusalem. You are witnesses of all this. Look! I am sending the promise of my Father upon you. Stay here in the city until you are clothed with power from above."

Then he led them out to Bethany, raised his hands and blessed them. As he blessed them he was taken into the heavens. They worshipped him. Then they returned to Jerusalem with great joy, continually going to the temple to praise God.

The disciples who met Jesus on the road to Emmaus returned to find that "the Eleven and the rest of the company had assembled." Jesus' mother, Mary, was probably one of that "company." Put yourself in Mary's place and let the events of verses 35-53 happen to you—as Mary. Tell Jesus how you feel. You, as Mary, are commissioned to bring forgiveness to people. How will Mary do that?

When has Mary interceded for you, to bring you God's forgiveness? How and for whom will you intercede, not only in prayer, but also in action, by your words, your acceptance, your offering of comfort?

Exercises

A Gospel is good news about Jesus Christ. It is not history, not biography. If you were an evangelist, how would you write the story of Jesus in order to attract others to him? What good news about him would you focus on?

It has been a while since you wrote a gospel as an activity in the Jesus chapter. You are different now. Take five minutes to remember the gospel stories. Which ones speak good news to you personally? No checking the text. Remembering is the key.

Now, for the next fifteen minutes, write a brief gospel. As you put down your pen at the end, pay attention to how you feel. Share your gospel out loud; then share your feelings. In order to keep within time limits you may have to subdivide your group.

Later, alone, compare your two gospels. What are the similarities, what are the differences? What do they mean?

Plan to serve coffee and cake to your group tonight. Leave two chairs empty. Read Luke 14:12-14.

> Jesus said to his host: "When you give a party do not just invite your friends, relatives, or rich neighbors. They will only return the invitation and so you will be repaid. When you give a party, ask the poor, the crippled, the lame and the blind. You will find happiness. These people have no means of repaying you."

Then invite Jesus to come to your circle and to bring one of his friends. Let each member of the group name Jesus' friend, someone or some type of person we despise or disdain. For example, I might say, "Jesus is bringing a military dictator with him here tonight." Leave silent time for the group to image Jesus and the dictator seating themselves with the group. Let the group pray silently for a few minutes.

The next person might suggest a homosexual or an ex-convict or a white-collar criminal. After the experience, ask the group how each felt. There may be anger expressed, or indignation: "Surely Jesus wouldn't bring such and such a character with him!" Don't argue or defend, just listen and receive. St. Paul warns us that Jesus is a scandal.

I briefly treat two stories, that of the sinful woman washing Jesus' feet and that of the woman bent for eighteen years. Your group can explore so much more deeply God's revelation of compassion from these incidents. Read Luke 7:36-50 aloud. Then reread it. This time pause every few verses and let anyone share an insight or feeling which the lines trigger. Don't worry about silences.

Use the same technique on Luke 13:10-17, although you may want to save it for another meeting. This is not really discussion, let alone argument. You can build on each other's comments but not contradict.

8. Jesus As God-Come-Close: John's Gospel

In this Gospel once again we learn that God takes the initiative, inviting us very close. "In the beginning was the Word." From the beginning God has tried to communicate to us all that God is. "In various and fragmented ways, God spoke through the prophets... but in these days God has spoken through a Son" (Hebrews 1:1-2). In times past the law "given through Moses" was God's self-expression. "Now grace and truth have come through Jesus Christ" (John 1:16-17). Grace and truth are the translations of *hesed* and *'emet*. God who showered people with *hesed* and *'emet* throughout their stormy history offers the final, total gift to them: God's own self in the flesh.

Jesus embodies, lives out in his body, God's *hesed* and *'emet*. God's inner life is spelled out for us by the outward life of Jesus. "No one has ever seen God, but the Son, who is closest to the Father's heart, he has made God known" (John 1:18). The center of John's writing, then, is God, but God made visible in the human life of Jesus— God communicated to us by the abiding life of the Spirit, the Paraclete. We will first focus on Jesus as John and his community understood him; then we will reflect on the work of the Paraclete.

130

Over the decades, from the time John the Evangelist knew Jesus in the flesh until later members of John's community put the finishing touches on the Fourth Gospel and John's First Epistle, many ideas about Jesus, many Christologies, were current in the various Christian communities. Like Luke, John understood Jesus as a prophet, but one greater than Moses; Jesus was portrayed as king, as shepherd, as vine. Of all the Christologies found in John's Gospel, for purposes of space we will only attend to Jesus as revealer and agent of God.

Jesus, The Embodiment of God

If we want to know what God is like, the Johannine community insists, we need only look at the historical life of Jesus. The Word of God made flesh is the perfect expression of God. The Latin root of the word incarnation, *carne*, means flesh. More than any other evangelist, John portrays Jesus as divine, yet John also portrays him as more deeply human, more "fleshy," than the others. Jesus is capable of passion, that deep and sustained emotion which so characterizes our humanity. Three incidents will illustrate the point. We can see his fear, his frustrated fury and his tenderness.

Jesus has delivered a "hard saying" about eating and drinking his body and blood. Even his disciples walk away from him muttering. That most painful of human emotions, one that erodes our basic trust, wells up in Jesus. He is afraid to be abandoned. Then he turns to the Twelve: "Will you also go away?" (John 6:59-71). In the past how often God questioned that fickle people, Israel, about their loyalties. Now Jesus asks the question in a simple, unmistakable way. God's fidelity, *'emet*, will last forever regardless of our walking away. Jesus embodies God's fidelity here, feeling in his human heart the pain of possible desertion. He is afraid.

God hates all that oppresses. Indeed, the Jewish Scriptures constantly record God's combat against forces of evil, alienation, injustice. Jesus puts flesh on this yearning of God to smash evil once for all. Death is the symbol and experience of ultimate evil. Jesus goes to Lazarus' tomb and there both groans in hatred of death and weeps in compassion with Mary of Bethany (John 11:38-44). God's own *hesed* and *'emet* are embodied there at the grave. Jesus groans in anger and grief.

Finally, Jesus is tender. God's extravagant love, *hesed*, has always been at the service of the people. Perhaps no other Gospel story so dramatically shows Jesus imaging God's own tenderness to us as the foot washing scene at the Last Supper.

Perhaps no other gospel experience for the majority of us so captures our tragic flaw: like Peter, we do not want to be served. We will be in control, whether over our dirty feet or our complex lives. In his Pulitzer-prize winning book, *Denial of Death*, Ernst Becker lays bare our refusal to be creature. The incident between Jesus and Peter exposed this root sin long ago. Peter will not receive the love and service of God, incarnated in the service, the tenderness of Jesus' action. To refuse to receive is to deny who we are, to deny our dependence on God's care.

Why is it important for us to take the incarnation so seriously? Because it is the closest God can come. Through the incarnation Jesus teaches us to reverence our own *carne*, our flesh, to appreciate God's action in and through our bodies, our emotions. God continues to take flesh in us, who are the body of Christ today. We are the ones called to embody God's *hesed* and *'emet* today. We do that not only through our minds and wills but through our bodies in all their glory and with all their limitations. Biblical spirituality and incarnational spirituality are two sides of the same coin.

Finally, we might also call Jesus the sacrament of God, a sign of God's presence and activity in the world. A sacrament "is an outward sign...which gives grace." Jesus is a sign of God who gives grace. He comes that we might have life, God's own life, and have it in abundance (John 10:10). Jesus is translucent. To look at Jesus is to see through him to God. Unlike the other Gospels, in John's Gospel there is no scene of transfiguration on Mount Tabor. Instead, the whole of Jesus' life and death is full of light and glory, the very light and glory of God.

Jesus, Agent of the Father

In John's Gospel Jesus is portrayed as agent of the Father. As the expression and embodiment of God, Jesus represents God in the flesh. John characterizes God's agent, Jesus, as both disciple and apostle.

Some Jewish background is important here. In Jesus' time there was a Jewish missionary thrust throughout the cities of the Roman empire. Prominent rabbis in Israel trained disciples to carry their message to distant lands. Disciples not only were to memorize the words of their teacher but were to imitate the rabbi in everything: dress, walk, table manners, laugh. Thus when a disciple arrived in a distant spot, the rabbi himself was present through his agent.

Jesus, in John's Gospel, is the disciple of his Father, continually learning. He does nothing on his own, but only what he sees his Father doing (5:19). He speaks nothing but what he hears from his Father (14:24). He does only the works of his Father (5:1-7). He reveals all the Father has revealed to him (15:15). As disciple (Latin: *discipulus/a*, learner) Jesus has learned from God and, more than merely imitating God, embodies God's work in the world.

An agent not only learns from the master teacher but then is sent on mission. Throughout the Fourth Gospel Jesus refers to his being sent from God. In Greek, the one "sent" is *apostolos*. Jesus is apostle. He is sent to bring life, "life in abundance" (10:10), sent to teach the truth that sets us free (8:31-32), sent to offer the love the Father has offered him (15:9), sent to create friendship by sharing everything he knows and is, everything he has received from his Father (8:42). Jesus is sent to bring acceptance (the Samaritan woman, chapter 4), healing (the man born blind, chapter 9), forgiveness (20:23), the good news that we are loved (3:16). As missioned by the Father Jesus offers peace "not as the world gives" (14:27) and joy, "that your joy may be full" (16:24). Without a doubt, however, Jesus' greatest gift is the Spirit.

The Paraclete

The fourth evangelist calls the Spirit the Paraclete, sometimes translated as comforter, counselor, advocate. From its Greek roots, *para-kaleo*, however, Paraclete means one who calls another forward. The priest-poet Gerard Manley Hopkins in a Pentecost sermon used the image of the Paraclete as a sports coach, urging us on as we round the bases, calling: "Come on, come on, you can do it!"

In the Last Supper discourse, that long and intimate conversation of Jesus and his friends, Jesus is concerned that we not be left orphans after his death. He describes how the Paraclete will act in his stead and on our behalf. As an abiding, comforting presence, the Spirit will live in us (14:17). From deep within us, the Paraclete will teach us everything and call to our minds Jesus' own teaching (14:26). Jesus calls the Paraclete the Spirit of truth who will witness to Jesus, just as his friends will find courage to witness (15:26-27). The Spirit of truth will convict the world of its evil, and will be the way we can discern good and evil (16:8-11). As Jesus learned from the Father, so the Spirit "will not speak on its own authority, but will tell only what the Spirit hears, revealing things that are to come." In fact, Jesus promises that the Paraclete will guide us into all truth (16:13). The Spirit will draw everything from Jesus in order to teach us, and in that way will glorify Jesus (16:14).

After such emphasis on the Spirit of truth in the Fourth Gospel's long Last Supper discourse, we may lose sight of Jesus' more intimate promise of the Spirit. Earlier, in the temple, Jesus cries out with eager longing:

> "If anyone is thirsty, let that one come to me. Whoever believes in me, let that one drink. As Scripture says, 'Streams of living water will flow out from within.'" Jesus was speaking of the Spirit whom believers in him would receive later; for the Spirit had not yet been given because Jesus had not yet been glorified (John 7:38-39).

The Spirit is like a fountain of living water, welling up from deep within us, soothing, healing, satisfying our various thirsts. The gentle and intimate flow of the Spirit, promised here, is fulfilled on Easter night. Jesus breathes on his disciples, inviting them to receive the Holy Spirit, who will be the ultimate instrument of peace and forgiveness of sin (20:21-23).

In John's Gospel the Father, Son and Paraclete are central. God initiates dialogue, relationship. We respond to the outpouring of God's unconditional love and fidelity, this "grace upon grace" received from the fullness of Jesus himself (John 1:16).

The fourth evangelist offers us a way to respond: "This is the work which God wants: believe in the one God has sent" (John 6:29). The evangelist writes his Gospel that we might believe (John 20:31). John's purpose blends with Jesus' purpose. Jesus in John's Gospel prays that we might be one and dies that we might be one, united with him and with each other. Let us first attend to John's purpose: to lead us to believe; and then to Jesus' purpose: to effect unity among believers.

Faith and Unity

For the Jews, believing was not intellectual assent to divinely revealed truths. It was not ascribing to untainted doctrine or absolute truth. Believing for John and his community was wholehearted attachment to God and to Jesus. Belief called for a basic trust in God's fidelity and subsequent commitment. Believing was not a habit or virtue of the mind so much as it was a habit of will and affection.

To respond to God's initiating love made tangible in Jesus was to be attracted to Jesus, to know him, to be his disciples, to be sent with him as apostles. To believe in Jesus was to cling to him, to be intimately united with him, to share mind and heart with him, to be committed to him. To believe is to accept Jesus' claim on our mind, our wills, our emotions, our bodies, our whole lives.

In this Gospel we notice how Jesus attracts people, literally draws them to himself. If Jesus is lifted up, John repeatedly tells us, he will draw all people to himself. To attract means, from its Latin origins, to draw. Throughout this Gospel, Jesus draws people. In the Gospel's opening scene at the Jordan River, Jesus invites John the Baptist's disciples to "come and see" where he lives (1:38). Andrew brings Peter, and Philip brings Nathaniel to this attractive new rabbi. The Pharisee Nicodemus risks his status to speak with Jesus by night; sparked by that dialogue (3:1-15), Nicodemus' courage grows (7:51) until finally his attraction to Jesus is so complete that he boldly asks Pilate for Jesus' dead body (19:39-41).

The Samaritan woman is drawn to him (John 4) as is Martha (John 11), for the evangelist makes it obvious that Jesus respects women's ability to discuss and comprehend theology. The Twelve are attached to him although others walk away (6:66-68). The Beloved Disciple's attraction pulls him even to Calvary. Only in John's Gospel is Mary, his mother, drawn to the cross. Only in John's Gospel do we find Jesus' two dear friends clinging to him (Mary Magdalene—20:10-18) and jumping overboard (Peter—21:4-8) to express their joy at his resurrection.

In times of crisis too, Jesus attracts: at Cana (2:1), in the storm at sea (6:16-21), feeding the hungry with loaves and fish (6:1-13). No one who comes to him will be cast out (6:37). Instead, "the whole world has gone after him" (12:19). When even the Greeks are attracted to him (12:20-21), Jesus knows that his hour has come. The arrival of these non-Jews signals that in "his hour," in being lifted up on the cross, Jesus literally has drawn all people to himself.

All these gospel characters are drawn to Jesus that they might receive the life in abundance which he was sent to bring. Life, life which lasts forever, is this, Jesus explains at the Last Supper: to know the one true God and the one whom God has sent (17:3). To come to Jesus is to know God, not only by the workings of our minds, but, as the Jews used the word, by the attachment of our hearts. To know is to be intimately united with. Like the gospel characters, we can be drawn to "the way, the truth and the life" who is Jesus (14:6). He promises that if we make his word our home, we will be his disciples—that is, we will learn from him, we will know the truth, and the truth will set us free (8:31-32).

Then we, like the gospel characters, we who have been drawn to him will be sent away. Notice how Andrew rushes off to bring Peter, Philip to find Nathaniel, the Samaritan woman to speak to her townspeople,

Martha to call her sister Mary, Mary Magdalene to tell the brothers that Jesus has risen. To be a disciple, to know truth, to be set free impels us to share that good news with others. To be a disciple will necessarily lead to being an apostle, one sent. All of this—being attracted, knowing, being sent—spells out what John means when he writes this Gospel so that we may believe and, through believing, have life (20:31).

John depicts Jesus, always hungry for what God wants (4:34), with his own desires on the night before he dies: "That they all may be one as we are one...Father, as you are in me and I am in you, that they may be one in us" (17:12-21). Mark, Matthew, Luke and Paul suggest other meanings for the death of Jesus, but John and his community spell out their understanding in terms of unity. Jesus died "to gather into one family all the scattered children of God" (11:52).

When he is lifted up on the cross, Jesus draws every believer to himself, uniting us all in his centrifugal force. Just as he united, while hanging on the cross, Mary his mother with the Beloved Disciple, so he unites believers through the centuries, creating us as new family, his family, that we may be one in him.

Guided Prayer

John 17:3

> "This is eternal life—to know you, the one true (faithful) God and Jesus Christ whom you have sent."

To the Jews, to study Scripture is to worship. When have you felt united with God as you listened to or read or studied Scripture? Let your memory stay with that experience. What feelings arise in you? Share those feelings with the Lord.

John 7:36

"I will give you fountains of living water welling up from deep within you."

What blocks you from living life in its abundance? Is there a boulder blocking that fountain within you, blocking the spring of living water? Speak with Jesus about your blocks. Where is his living water stagnant in your life? What do you want from him now?

John 11:20-28

When Martha heard that Jesus was coming (long after she had summoned him because her brother Lazarus was dying), she went out to meet him. Mary sat at home. Martha said to Jesus, "Lord, if you had been here, my brother would not have died. I know, even now, that anything you ask of God, God will give you."

Jesus said to her, "Your brother will rise." Martha replied, "I know he will rise, in the resurrection on the last day." Then Jesus said, "I am the resurrection and the life. Whoever believes in me, should that person die, that person will really live. Everyone who lives and believes in me will never die. Do you believe this?" She replied, "Yes, Lord. I have come to believe that you are the anointed one, the Son of God, the one who is coming into the world."

When she had said this, she called Mary, her sister, and took her aside, saying, "The Master is here and is asking for you...."

Martha is an initiator. She has an adult relationship

with Jesus. How does Martha relate to your personality? How does Jesus feel about her? How does he feel about the Martha in you and/or in those around you?

John 11:48-52

> The Sanhedrin was saying, "If we leave Jesus alone, everyone will come to believe in him. Then the Romans will come and take away our land and our nation." One of them, Caiaphas, high priest that year, said, "You know nothing. Consider: It is better for you that one man should die instead of the people, so that the whole nation might not be destroyed."

> He did not say this on his own. As high priest for that year, he told that Jesus was going to die for the nation, and for more than the nation. Jesus was going to die to gather into one family all the scattered children of God.

Jesus died to gather all the scattered children of God. In what ways are you scattered? pulled apart? not whole? not integrated? Ask Jesus to gather you. Where in your families, communities, world interests do you need the attractiveness of Jesus and the power released through his death to gather people together? Pray for these situations.

Then contemplate Jesus. Ask him if it is worth his dying. Ask him why gathering his people was so important to him. Keep a mental image of Jesus on the cross with the peoples of all nations and times—and yourself—coming to him. Ask him how he feels. Respond to his feelings.

John 13:3-9

> Fully aware that the Father had put everything into his power, aware that he had come from God

and was going to God, Jesus rose from the supper table and took off his outer garment. Than taking a towel and tying it around his waist, he poured water into a basin and began to wash the feet of his disciples. He would dry them with the towel around his waist.

He came to Simon Peter, who said to him, "Master, are you going to wash my feet?" Jesus answered, "You don't understand now what I am doing. You will understand later." Peter said, "You will never wash my feet." Jesus replied, "Unless I wash you, you will have no part with me." Simon Peter then said to him, "Master, wash not only my feet but my head and my hands as well!"

Peter refuses to be served. He cannot believe that Jesus could love him that much. Jesus wants to kneel before you, he wants to serve you. How do you feel about that desire of his? Talk with him about it.

John 14:23-26

At his last supper, Jesus said, "Whoever loves me will live in my word. My Father will love that person. We will come and dwell deep within such a person. Whoever does not love me does not live in my word. The word you hear, however, is not mine, but the word of the Father who sent me. I have told you this while I am with you. The Paraclete, the Holy Spirit whom the Father will send in my name, will teach you everything. The Paraclete will call to your minds everything I told you."

Friends teach one another. Who are the best teachers you ever had? What made them good teachers? What in you made you able to learn from them? What did they

touch in you? What did you open to them? Jesus has
called you to learn of him, to know him. What are you
most glad he has taught you? What do you want him to
teach/touch in you now: senses? heart? feelings? desires?
intellect? memory? Talk to him as your teacher/friend.

John 15:14-17; 14:15-18

> At his last supper, Jesus said, "You are my
> friends if you do what I command you (to love one
> another as I have loved you). I no longer call you
> servants because a servant does not know what the
> master is doing. I have called you friends because
> everything I have learned from God I have shared
> with you. You did not choose me. I chose you. I
> have appointed you to go and bear fruit which will
> last.... This I command you: love one another.
>
> "If you love me you will keep my command-
> ment. I will ask the Father, and God will give you
> another Paraclete to be with you always, the Spirit
> of truth.... You will know the Spirit because it re-
> mains with you, will be in you. I am not leaving
> you orphans."

You are the one whom Jesus calls "friend." His
whole life expresses his consuming desire to be with you.
Now he promises you his own Spirit, not just to be with
you but to live (be alive, moving) within you. Hear his
promise ring within you. How do you feel about his
desire to share your life? Tell Jesus what it means to you
to have him be so intimately present to you. What do you
want to share with him? You are sent, too, to share your
life and spirit with one other, five others, fifty others. To
whom are you sent? How do you feel about being sent?
Talk with Jesus about these feelings.

John 16:12-13

At his last supper, Jesus continued, "I have so much more to tell you, but you cannot bear it now. When the Spirit of truth comes, the Spirit will guide you into all truth...."

Guided not simply *to* truth, to stand outside and look, but you will be guided *into* truth, so you may live, make your home in truth. You are promised truth to set you free. What is your deepest experience of freedom? Relish that freedom now with Jesus and his Spirit. How were you brought to that freedom? Who was the human instrument or what was the historical event which helped you to freedom? What about now? Is there something in your life nagging you, binding you? How Jesus wants to free you! Plead with Jesus' Spirit (your Advocate) to glorify Jesus in you by setting you free.

You are sent, too, to help others become more free, to be the instrument of Jesus' freeing action. Talk with Jesus about what you can do to foster more freedom in your community, among your friends and co-workers.

John 15:1-12

At his last supper, Jesus said, "I am the true vine and my Father is the farmer.... Remain in me as I remain in you. No branch can bear fruit unless it remains on the vine. So neither can you unless you remain in me. Whoever lives in me, and I in that person, will bear much fruit. Without me, you can do nothing.... As the Father loves me, so I also love you. Live on in my love....

"I have told you all this so that my joy might be in you and your joy might be complete. This is my commandment: love one another as I love you."

Jesus deeply, passionately desires that you be in union with him. In some manuscripts, verse 11 reads: "so that my joy may be in you," and others read: "so that I may have joy in you." Can you believe that second reading? Listen to Jesus speak directly to you, tell you that you are the cause of his joy. How do you feel? Speak with him about these feelings. How can you pass on the life you receive from the true vine, Jesus? To whom will you hand on life in abundance today?

John 17:1-3, 6-11

> When Jesus had finished speaking at his last supper, he raised his eyes to heaven and prayed, "Father, the hour has come. Give glory to your son so that your son may give glory to you. Just as you gave him authority over all people, so may he give eternal life to all whom you gave him. This is eternal life: to know you, the one true God, and the one whom you sent, Jesus Christ....
>
> "I revealed you to those whom you gave me...and they have kept your word.... I pray for them...because they are yours. Everything of mine is yours and everything of yours is mine.... I am coming to you, Holy Father. Keep them in yourself so that they may be one, just as we are one...."

You are in the Last Supper room, seeing, hearing, smelling, perhaps tasting the remains of the meal. Jesus stands up and begins to pray. Whom among your family and friends do you want Jesus to pray for, to unite?

Read again (perhaps aloud) Jesus' prayer. When you have finished, go over to where Jesus is standing. What do you want to tell him in these few last moments of life?

John 21:1-13

> Risen, Jesus revealed himself again to his dis-

ciples at the Sea of Tiberias in this way. To those gathered—Thomas, Nathaniel, Zebedee's sons, and two other disciples—Simon Peter said, "I am going fishing." They said, "We will come with you." So they got into the boat but all that night they caught nothing.

At dawn, Jesus was standing on the shore, but they did not realize it was Jesus. He said to them, "Children, have you caught anything to eat?" They replied, "No." So he said, "Throw the net over the right side of the boat and you will find something." So they threw it over and then were not able to pull it in, so great were the number of fish.

The disciple whom Jesus loved said to Peter, "It is the Lord." When Simon Peter heard that, he put on his garment, for he was naked, and then jumped into the sea. The rest of the disciples came in the boat, dragging the net with the fish.

When they climbed out on shore, they noticed a charcoal fire with fish on it, and some bread. Jesus said: "Bring some of the fish you have caught." So Peter went over and dragged the net ashore, full of large fish. Even with 153 of them the net was not torn. Then Jesus invited them, "Come and eat breakfast...." Jesus came to them, took bread and gave it to them. He did the same with the fish.

Imagine this scene. Smell the water, the fish; see the colors of dawn, the glow of the charcoal fire, etc. Do you identify better with Peter or with the one whom Jesus loved? Do you recognize Jesus in your life? Do you "jump in" at once just to be with him or are you hesitating to get close to him?

He is very much alive. He wants to feed you, to serve you. How do you feel about that? Tell him.

Exercises

We find rich and earthy symbols in John's Gospel. Read the Cana story aloud (2:1-11). Then in silence ask each member of your group to sip a glass of water. Next, ask them to sip a glass of wine (have some grape juice on hand should someone prefer it). After about 10-15 minutes of silent tasting, share what these symbols said to you.

Another time, the group might spend ten minutes in silent contemplation of a candle (or, perhaps, a fire in a fireplace). Then share feelings and insights on Jesus as light. A vine or philodendron plant could lead to contemplation of Jesus as the true vine and ourselves as branches.

Wash one another's feet. Share feelings about it afterward. Why is it so difficult for so many of us to receive service, care, affection? What do you want to do about your discomfort, hesitations and fears?

9. From Fear to Faith and Freedom

To introduce the teaching of Paul, one for whom God came very close, we will study his letter to the Galatians. One of Paul's earliest, Galatians is also one of his most autobiographical letters. In it, while coping with urgent problems presented by the young Christians from Galatia, Paul presents himself as one who is chosen, missioned and free.

God has taken the initiative in Paul's life—but only after Paul had struggled for control, not only of his life but also of his salvation. Paul worked to save himself by means of the law. Then, one day on the road to Damascus, this zealous Pharisee met the risen Lord, who turned his heart and mind around. A change of mind, or *metanoia* in Greek, is often translated "conversion" in English. Paul however was not converted from a life of wickedness, nor from Judaism to Christianity. Paul was converted from his attitude of self-righteousness. Jesus set him free from needing to prove himself to God. God already loved him, and had chosen him from his mother's womb.

Chosen, Missioned and Free

In his conversion experience Paul learned that to persecute Christians is actually to persecute Christ (Acts 9:4). Paul thus found that in Christ he was in solidarity with others, whether Jew or Gentile, slave or free, male or female (Galatians 3:28). He was missioned to them, particularly to the Gentiles, and he esteemed slaves and women because they too were "in Christ."

To be missioned is to be sent, *apostello* in Greek (apostle). Paul considered himself an apostle. The first two chapters of this letter defend his identity as an apostle.

For Luke, the author of Acts, an apostle is a male who has walked with Jesus from the time of his baptism in the Jordan (Acts 1:21-22). There are only twelve because that number is symbolic for Luke of the twelve tribes of God's *new* chosen people, a new Israel who is the Christian community.

Paul's criteria for what constitutes an apostle differ. An apostle, according to Paul, is one who has experienced that Christ is risen, alive, and present. An apostle is then missioned by Christ (1 Corinthians 15). We cannot qualify for apostleship according to Luke's criteria, but according to Paul's we do. Every Christian is chosen to be an apostle.

To be baptized is to be an apostle. Once we believed that the lay apostolate was our participation in the work of the bishops, successors to the apostles. Once we believed that we had a mission and ministry in the Church only because the bishops and priests invited us to share their ministry. In these days we have rediscovered how baptism anoints us to share Christ's own identity, mission and ministry. We, the laity, have a mission and ministry because we all are the Church.

Chosen and missioned by God, Paul receives a new freedom. Some twenty years after his conversion, in his Letter to the Galatians Paul proclaims again and again his core experience: Christ has set us free from the law (Galatians 5:1).

Salvation is God's gift freely given, not a reward for our good behavior. When Paul preached this good news of freedom, the Galatians accepted the Gospel.

After Paul moved on, however, some Judaizers, Christians who were Jewish by race, arrived in the Galatian community. They, who were to trouble Paul during most of his apostolic life, insisted that Gentile Christians had to be circumcised and keep the Jewish law. Judaizing Christians taught the new Gentile converts that they had missed a step. They first had to become Jews. Paul's anger in this letter is directed both at those Judaizing Christian missionaries and at the Galatians, who trusted their law-centered rather than Christ-centered teaching.

Adult Morality

In insisting that Christians are free from the law of the Jews, Paul is hardly preaching immoral or amoral behavior. He realizes that children need rules and regulations to build habits of discipline (Galatians 3:24-25). Law-centered morality, a kind of taboo mentality which fears and avoids punishment, may be normal for children but not for us who are mature Christians. According to this letter's theme, Christ has set us free from the law and all the taboos and guilt associated with it. In other words, our faith in Christ leads us to an adult morality.

Faith means our attachment to Christ, our welcome of his claim on our entire lives. Adult morality springs not from fear but from faith, our loving response to God's first having loved us. God initiates our salvation, lavishing love and faithfulness. Our response of love and fidelity to God/Christ/Spirit is free and freeing, truly an adult morality.

In this letter Paul indicates how he has responded in adult fashion to God's choice of him. He is obedient, concerned for the poor, prayerful and united with Christ. He is not afraid to submit his ideas to dialogue with authority (Galatians 2:2, 9). Being in union with the other apostles is more important to him than any righteous proclamation of truth as he alone sees it.

Converted from self-righteousness, Paul has learned a new kind of obedience. He has given up, as proper to a child, the slavish, fearful adherence to law and regulations. His adult obedience means an open listening, an obedience based on dialogue in which he remains flexible and free. The apostles James, John and Cephas (Peter), support his mission to the Gentiles. They ask him to remember the poor which, indeed, Paul was eager to do (2:9-10).

As for ourselves, being freed from the law does not lead us to lawlessness but to a creative fidelity, to dialogue, to obedience. Being freed from the law, its demands and scrupulous self-centering, allows our energies to be devoted to service and care for the poor. Being freed from the law reminds us that it is Jesus who saves not our own works and merits.

In this early Letter Paul makes a profound statement which becomes a cornerstone of his theology. He is keenly aware that the Spirit lives and moves in his heart, crying "Abba! Father!" (4:6). That same Spirit, keeping him prayerfully united with God, is the source of his astounding experience: "It is no longer I who live, but Christ lives in me" (2:20).

This is the key to an adult morality. The Spirit moves us interiorly, transforming our lives gradually into an expression of Christ's own life, present and powerful today.

In Matthew's Gospel we are enjoined to see and to care for Christ in the least of our brothers and sisters

(Matthew 25). Some can see Christ in others, others cannot. Another way of responding to the risen Christ who is still present among us is Paul's: Christ is in us. Christ is at work, caring and healing and freeing and teaching and doing justice for the outcasts in and through us. Instead of seeing Christ in others, we are united with Christ alive within us.

This Pauline experience grounds the teaching of Pope Pius XII in his encyclical on the body of Christ. In 1943 the Pope wrote that we, the Church, the body of Christ, are Jesus Christ extended in space and time and communicated to humankind. The risen Lord is present and active through the presence and activity of every baptized Christian.

We make Jesus present to today's world, to our country, our neighborhood, community, family. We may be free from the law, but to offer our life in faith, to invite the Spirit to transform us into Christ, calls for a mature response, an adult morality. It calls for freedom. "For freedom, Christ has set you free. Let no one make you a slave again" (Galatians 5:1).

Guided Prayer

Galatians 1:1-16

Paul, an apostle, sent not from human authorities, but through Jesus Christ and God the Father, who raised him from the dead, and all those who are with me.

To the churches of Galatia:

Grace to you and peace from God our Father and the Lord Jesus Christ, who gave himself for our sins so that he might save us according to God's desire.

To God be glory forever and ever. Amen.

I am amazed that you are so quickly abandoning the one who called you, turning to a different gospel. There are some who pervert the gospel. If we or even an angel should proclaim or preach a gospel different from the one we first preached to you, let that one be cursed....

Do you think I am trying to win favor with human beings or with God? If I were trying to please people, I would not be Christ's servant. You must know, brothers and sisters, that the gospel I preach is not of human origin. I did not learn it from human authority but I was taught through a revelation of Jesus Christ.

You have heard how I persecuted the church of God, trying to destroy it. My Judaism had become fanatical beyond that of my colleagues, since I was so overly zealous for the old ways, traditions of my ancestors.

Then God who had set me apart from my mother's womb and called me through grace was pleased to reveal the Son to me so that I might proclaim him to all the nations, especially to those who were not Jews....

The Lord set Paul apart from birth to proclaim the Gospel to the Gentiles. Reflect on God's choosing you "from your mother's womb." When, where, how has this choosing continued throughout your life? Tell God how you feel about this choice.

Galatians 2:15-3:2

We who are Jews by birth, not sinners from among the Gentiles, know that a person is not justified, set right with God, by works of the law. Not by keeping the law but by believing in Jesus Christ, are we justified. By works of the law, no one is set right with God....

Through the law I died to law, that I might begin to live for God. I have been crucified with Christ. So I live, no longer I, but Christ lives in me. In my flesh I live by faith in the Son of God, who has loved me and given himself up for me. I never want the grace of God to be set aside. If, however, we can be justified by keeping the law, then Christ died for nothing.

O foolish Galatians!... Did you receive the Spirit because you kept the law, or because you believed the good news?

Paul asks how the Galatians came to receive the Spirit. Was it through keeping the law or believing the Gospel message? How have you come to receive the Spirit? Why does God love you? Because you keep the commandments or because you let the Spirit transform you day by day into Jesus? Ask God what makes you so pleasing, such a delight to God.

Galatians 3:23-27

Before there was faith, we were confined under the law, waiting for the faith that was to be revealed. The law was our guardian, our trainer, preparing us for Christ, that we might be justified by faith. Now that faith has come, we no longer need that guardian, the law. Through faith you are all children of God in Christ Jesus. All of you who were baptized, plunged into Christ, have put on Christ.

In God's plan, we as youngsters learned and practiced the Jewish law. It was like a trainer, Paul writes.

Jesus has now called us to make adult decisions, to learn from him day by day how to cling to him (for Paul faith means attachment to Jesus). What is more satisfying to you: a set code which you thought established your security with God, or a growing relationship with God's Son which gives you another kind of security? Be honest as you discuss this with God. The law does make us secure. We may have to beg Christ to help us find all our security in him, not in law.

Galatians 3:28

In Christ there is neither Jew nor Gentile, neither slave nor free person, neither male nor female.

Can you remember a time when you felt insulted or discriminated against? Remember the incident as vividly as possible. See the people involved; hear them; re-feel your emotions at the time. Then stop. Watch Jesus walk into the situation. What does he do, say? To you, to the other(s)? How can you respond to him? Pray for the gift of reconciliation in your personal life, for the healing of memories. Then pray to have all divisions among peoples, racism, classism, sexism, nationalism, removed from you and from our Church around the world.

Galatians 5:1-8, 12

For freedom Christ has set us free. Let no one make you a slave again. I tell you, if you get yourself circumcised (as the Judaizers insist), Christ will be of no help to you. If you are circumcised, remember you are bound to keep the entire law (613 commandments).

If you try to justify yourself by observing the law, you are cut off from Christ. You have fallen away from grace.

It is through the Spirit, by faith, that we wait in hope for righteousness. In Christ circumcision counts for nothing. All that counts is faith, working through love.

You were on the right track. Who blocked you from obeying the truth? That enticement to security does not come from the One who called you.... Would that the knife of those who are disturbing you about circumcision would slip and they would castrate themselves!

Mortal sin means that we choose to cut ourselves off completely from Christ. What does Paul call "mortal sin" in this section? How do you feel about that? Discuss it with Jesus. Ask him if Paul is wrong. Remember that freedom is frightening and risky and calls for response-ability. The freedom offered us by Jesus calls for an hour-by-hour response to him, made flesh in his people.

Galatians 5:1

For freedom Christ has set you free. Let no one make you a slave again.

In the past, who or what has enslaved you? How were you set free? How does the memory make you feel? Tell the risen Lord about your memories and feelings. Ask him (not yourself) where he still wants to free you.

Galatians 6:2

Bear one another's burdens and so you will fulfill the law of Christ.

What is the law of Christ? How do we keep it? Ask for the fullness of the Spirit, who is love and burden-bearer. The Spirit is your power to love, living deep within you. Share with the Spirit some of your burdens in loving.

Galatians 5:13-25

> You were called to freedom, brothers and sisters. Do not use this freedom as license, but rather to serve one another in love. The whole law is summed up in: Love your neighbor as yourself....
>
> Walk in the Spirit and so you will not yield to the desires of the flesh which oppose the Spirit. If you are led by the Spirit, you are not under the law.
>
> Works of the flesh are obvious: impurity, drunkenness and orgies; idolatry and magic; hatreds, rivalries, jealousy acted upon; outburst of rage; acts of selfishness, dissensions and factions....
>
> In contrast, the fruit which the Spirit produces is love, joy, peace, patience, kindness, generosity, faithfulness, gentleness and self-control. There is no law to regulate these.... Living in the Spirit, let us then walk in the Spirit.

Use Galatians 5:22, the fruits of the Spirit, as a criterion to judge your actions and to make your decisions. Do the decisions you make help you to grow in peace, joy, love, kindness, and so forth? Remember a major decision you made this past year. Ask the risen Lord to show you how these fruits of the Spirit have blossomed through your decision.

After some activity, later today, stop and read Galatians 5:22 again. What fruits of the Spirit were operating in that activity? How do you feel about that? After some decision you make today, stop and again read 5:22. What fruits did you experience after making that decision? How will you respond to the Spirit?

Exercises

Brainstorm together a list of taboos. No discussion is allowed in brainstorming. List religious, cultural (like table manners), or family (like putting the toilet seat down) taboos. Then reflect in silence: what taboos have you outgrown? What taboos has Jesus freed you from?

After reflection time, share with your group those new freedoms you have experienced. Choose those which are appropriate to the level of trust in your group. After the sharing, get in touch with how you feel as you listen to the others' stories of freedom. Be careful not to judge because the Spirit works uniquely with each person. If you care to, share your feelings with your group, and perhaps conclude with shared prayer.

What does Paul mean when he writes, "You who would be justified (saved) by the law, you are completely cut off from Christ, you have fallen away from grace" (Galatians 5:4)? In the Acts of the Apostles (15:9-11), Peter says to the Christian congregation that keeping the law is an impossible burden. Since the new Christians were saved by grace, not by the law, why impose the law on Gentile converts?, Peter asks. Salvation, according to Ephesians 2:4-10, is not a reward for any work we do but God's free gift.

Have you ever tried to win God's approval by doing good works? How can you believe that you already have God's approval, that God's love for you is unconditional, extravagant, faithful? Paul says the only law is to bear one another's burdens (Galatians 6:2).

What do you experience, believe, teach the next generation about law? Discuss, but keep it focused on your experience. You do not need to convince others but to hear your group work out for themselves the relationship between grace and law, faith and freedom.

If the discussion becomes argumentative, it helps to keep a minute of silence after each person speaks. In that minute, united with the teacher-Spirit, members can really hear what the speaker said. The atmosphere will become contemplative.

What apostolic work have you done in the past? We tend to call apostolate (our being sent) "ministry," another word for service. What would you name as your ministry within the Christian community? What is your ministry to the secular world? Would you want your present ministry recognized by the community in a formal way (a commissioning service or even an ordination)? Why or why not?

What future needs of the Church do you envision? What gifts do you have which could fill those needs? What do you envision your future ministry to be? Discuss.

10. Dying and Rising: The Mystery of a Community's Faith

In his letters to the Corinthians, Paul sets forth the mystery of faith: Jesus in action, for us. We proclaim it in every Eucharist: Christ has died, Christ is risen and Christ not only will come again but remains active in his mission and ministry through his body, the Church.

In the First Letter to the Corinthians we will pay attention to what underpins Paul's theology—the cross and resurrection. Through the paschal mystery, that is, the dying and rising of Jesus, we are united as community and gifted for the community.

In Paul's Second Letter to the Corinthians we will see how Jesus' death and resurrection challenges us to compassion and to transformation. Because the dying and rising of Jesus brought about our reconciliation, we are commissioned to be God's ambassadors of reconciliation. Finally, we will turn to the person of Paul himself, accused by so many of us as arrogant, but pronouncing himself a weakling through whom God's power can operate.

Cross, Resurrection and Community

Paul always maintained that the resurrection of Jesus was crucial to Christianity. "If Christ is not risen, then our faith is in vain" (1 Corinthians 15:14). It made no difference to him that he had never met Jesus face to face, in the flesh, that he had never met the historical Jesus. Paul's core religious experience, first on the road to Damascus, was of the risen Christ, the Lord.

In 1 Corinthians 15, Paul explains how Jesus' resurrection signals the triumph of us all over death. Because some in the community at Corinth were so ecstatic about this good news of resurrection, Paul had to remind them that intimately linked with resurrection, however, is crucifixion. Jesus' bloody death on a cross was sheer stupidity to the Greeks, a real stumbling block to the Jews. Yet God brought victory out of a most humiliating, painful situation.

What flows from Jesus' death and resurrection is a new community. John the evangelist portrays this new community at the cross when Mary and the Beloved Disciple were given to each other (John 19); the Spirit, according to Luke, forms the new community for the sake of mission (Acts 1-2). Paul understands that when Jesus' death and resurrection are proclaimed, when we eat his body and drink his blood, we who are many are united as one (1 Corinthians 10-11). It is Jesus' body and blood handed over which calls us to hand ourselves over to each other.

The community which Paul founded at Corinth, however, was not committed to each other. When they came together to celebrate the Lord's supper and proclaim the Lord's death and resurrection, some came drunk, some came stingy with their potluck contribution. Instead of being eager to share their meal with the poor of the community, each one was gorging himself or herself and so insulting the body of Christ, the Church who is the poor. "You eat and drink condemnation of yourselves" (1 Corinthians 11:29).

Although the Corinthians may have used the "correct" sacred elements of bread and wine, their supper ritual was not Eucharist. Eucharist calls us to and nourishes us for justice and love.

So Paul spells out how to love the body of Christ, the Church. Greed and competition among community members could be healed if they would recognize that in their community were a variety of gifts, services and works. All these blessings are centered in and flowing from the Spirit. All are given for the common good (1 Corinthians 12:4-7). Of all the gifts, of course, the greatest is love (Chapter 13).

A Share in the Cross and Resurrection

Paul's Second Letter to the Corinthians is probably composed of a few letters, even a fragment which just doesn't seem to fit. Its contents, again so centered in Jesus' death and resurrection, reveal quite a bit about Paul's own share in the Lord's paschal (dying and rising) experience.

As Paul opens the letter, he is deeply afflicted. He finds in his emotional pain, however, not only God's comfort, but a new sensitivity and compassion toward all who suffer (1:3-7). Some of his suffering is disappointment with the community. He wavers between defensiveness and vulnerability, yet he always exalts God's power at work in him (3:4-6 and again in chapter 12). God's power expresses itself in the transformation of the Christian. The power of God, *dynamis*, is the Spirit who is also Lord. The Spirit leads us to freedom and transforms us from glory to glory (3:17-18).

Paul's experience, even in the terrible difficulties detailed in chapters 4 and 11, is freedom. He knows that he carries a treasure in his fragile, rough, earthenware self. He knows that if he carries the dying of Jesus in this broken, beaten and exhausted body of his, the power of Jesus' new and risen life also shines through his flesh (4:10-12).

The newness of the Lord's risen life has brought a new quality of life into this world. Paul calls each of us a new creation (5:17). What has caused such radical newness? Through the death and resurrection of Jesus, there is reconciliation, no more alienation. Barriers are broken. Right relationships are restored. We are no longer strangers to each other, but brothers and sisters who are entrusted by God to proclaim the good news of reconciliation (5:18-21).

Paul certainly practiced what he preached, trying to break down barriers between races, classes and sexes. "In Christ there is neither Gentile nor Jew, slave nor free, male nor female" (Galatians 3:28). Yet he found it difficult to deal with enemies in the mission field, the Judaizers of Galatians and the "super apostles" described in 2 Corinthians.

In the last four chapters of this second letter, Paul writes sarcastically about the "powers" of the super apostles who threaten his community at Corinth with dazzling displays of spiritual gifts. In these chapters Paul admits his various weaknesses. His experience is that when he is weakest he is most effective in mission because God's power can take over his prayer and life and work (12:1-10). In fact, he will boast of his weakness, united with the dying and rising of Christ.

> For he was crucified in weakness but lives by the power of God. We too are weak...but in dealing with you we shall live with him by the power of God (13:4).

Guided Prayer

When you take a period for prayer, begin by asking the Spirit to pray within you and to show you precisely how you have been gifted throughout your life. Ask the Spirit of truth to teach you that your gifts are unique, full of God's power, and needed for the building up of the whole Church-community.

1 Corinthians 1:21-25; 2:1-5

By means of the foolish message which we preach, God decided to save those who believe. Jews demand miracles for proof, Greeks insist on wisdom. Yet we preach Christ, and him crucified, a scandal to the Jews and foolishness to the Gentiles. For those whom God has called, both Jew and Gentile, Christ is the power of God and the wisdom of God. God's foolishness is wiser than human wisdom. God's weakness is stronger than human power....

When I came to you, my sisters and brothers, to preach God's truth, I did not use great learning and sophisticated language. While I was with you I decided to know only Jesus Christ and especially his death on the cross. So when I arrived to be with you I was weak and trembling with fear. You could be certain that my teaching and proclamation were not delivered with any skillful words of human wisdom, but with the convincing power of the Spirit. Thus your faith is not founded on human wisdom but on God's own power.

Look for a while at a crucifix. Is this foolishness? Is it weakness? How do you feel? Is it difficult to think of Jesus crucified? Why? Why not? Are you angry? Afraid? Depressed? Grateful? Wondering? (Remember: there are no wrong ways to feel, no emotions which are holier than others.) Talk over these feelings with Jesus. Read the passage again and respond.

1 Corinthians 12:4-13

There are a variety of gifts, but the same Spirit who gives them; there are many ways to serve, but one Lord is served; there are many kinds of work, but it is the same God who gives ability to each. The presence of the Spirit is shown in each of us for the good of all. The Spirit gives one person a message full of wisdom, while to another the Spirit gives a word of knowledge. The one Spirit gives faith to one, the power to heal to another, the ability to do mighty works to yet another. One receives the gift of proclaiming God's message, another the ability to discern which gifts are of the Spirit and which are not. The Spirit leads one to speak in tongues, and another to interpret these foreign words. It is one and the same Spirit who does all this, giving a unique gift to each person.

Christ is a single body. It has many different parts, yet it is one body. So all of us, whether Jews or Gentiles, whether slaves or free, have been baptized, plunged into one body by the one Spirit. We have all been given the same Spirit to drink.

What gifts has the Spirit given you? Try not to think and introspect. Let them bubble up from the Spirit (fountain of living water) and just listen. What is God's purpose in gifting you? Ask. Listen. Tell God how you feel about these gifts. Your gifts need not be limited to those from Paul's list. Laughter, common sense, money sense, awareness, ease and joy in cooking, woodworking, etc., are given for the building up of the body (your family, your community, your neighborhood, your country).

Think of someone you know who has a particular gift mentioned by Paul. How do you feel about that person? Tell the Spirit how proud you are of that person, or how jealous. Keep asking the Spirit (every day) to show you what your gifts are.

We cannot do all the good we would like to do in our lifetime—but our brothers and sisters all over the world are doing a variety of good works, building up the body. If we "welcome" them (accept, understand, appreciate their gifts and their ministry) we receive their reward (Matthew 10:40-41).

2 Corinthians 1:3-5

> Blessed be the God and Father of our Lord Jesus Christ, the Father of mercies, the God of all consolation. God comforts us in our afflictions, so that we are able to console those who have many troubles with the same comfort which we have received from God. Just as we have a share in Christ's many sufferings, so through Christ we share in God's great consolation.

Ask Jesus to help you remember difficult situations in the past month. How did your living through those difficulties lead you to grow in some small way in compassion for others? Ask to have the heart of Christ, so that you may comfort others in their sufferings. Pray for some of those who are suffering now. In Hebrew to pray means to stroke the face of God, a way to come very close.

2 Corinthians 3:17-18

> The Lord is the Spirit. Wherever the Spirit of the Lord is, there is freedom. All of us with our faces uncovered reflect the glory of the Lord. We are being transformed more and more into the likeness of the Lord, from glory to glory. Such is the influence of the Lord who is Spirit.

How has the Spirit influenced you through your

study of Scripture and your efforts at prayer? How have you been gradually transformed? How do you feel? Tell the Spirit what more you want. Remember that God wants to lavish on you all that God is, so ask.

2 Corinthians 4:6-11

God said: Let light shine out of the darkness! This same God made light shine in our hearts, leading us to know God's glory shining in the face of Christ. We hold this treasure in earthenware pots. This shows that power belongs to God and not to us.

As for us, we are troubled but not crushed; in doubt, but not in despair. We have many enemies but are never totally alone, and although badly hurt at times, we are not destroyed. At all times we carry in our bodies the dying of Jesus, so that the life of Jesus may be shown in this earthly flesh of ours.

How are the things you suffer like Jesus' agony and passion? When in the past has the life and resurrection joy of Jesus sprung from those very difficulties? Ask the Spirit to help you remember. Ask for the power of Christ's resurrection to become apparent in your life today. To be an attractive sign of Jesus alive is to be in mission.

2 Corinthians 5:16-l8, 21

We no longer judge anyone by human standards. If at one time we judged Christ by such standards, we no longer do so. When we are joined to Christ we are a new creation. The old person is gone and the new person is present. All this is done by God who, through Christ, was reconciling us, changing us from enemies to friends. God has given us the work of leading others to friendship, making us ambassadors of reconciliation....

For our sake Christ who was without sin was made sin. Then, in union with him, we now share the very holiness of God.

Only if we know how much we lack peace and unity in our hearts, our families, our country, can we appreciate what being reconciled means. Ask Jesus to show you where in your own heart or in your relationships you need reconciliation. Then read the passage again and respond to him.

2 Corinthians 12:7-10

To keep me from being puffed up with pride, I was given a "thorn in the flesh." Three times I prayed to the Lord about this, asking to have it taken away. Christ's answer was: My grace is enough for you. My power is most strong when you are weak.

So I am happy to boast of my weakness, in order to experience Christ's power. I can be content with weakness, insults, hardships, persecution, difficulties for Christ's sake. For when I am weak, then I am really strong.

God's power, *dynamis* in Greek, is the theme of this section. When have you seen this power at work in your weakness, frustration, failure? Remember hardships, being misunderstood or "persecuted." After looking at your life with Jesus, narrow it down to just this week's setbacks. Ask him to be strong in your weakness.

Reread this passage. Ask Jesus now to reveal times in your life when you were weak but his power was strong.

Exercises

This exercise is a reflection on the people in our life whom we call friends and community and thus Church. Draw a circle, two inches in diameter. Then draw another around it, then a third and a fourth circle. In the center circle list those people whom you would consider intimates, those whom you can completely trust. In the next outer circle list your friends, those with whom you have close bonds of affection. In the third circle, write the names of your companions, people you enjoy being with, those with whom you have a working relationship, perhaps some of your neighbors, your car pool or softball team. The outer-most circle is for your acquaintances, or at least some of them.

You need not show your circles to anyone, but in your group discuss what Christian community means, what church means. Is your community different from your family? your parish? Is your church smaller, closer than the diocese, the parish? Could friends and intimates who are not the same religious denomination be church for you? Why or why not?

Remember, the purpose of this discussion is to clarify our own values about church and to learn from others' viewpoints. It is not our responsibility to convince anyone of his or her errors, nor to prove our point. The Spirit can teach, can "guide into all truth," when we keep our minds open and do not force our version of truth.

Open your New Testaments to 1 Corinthians 13, the famous hymn of love. Have someone read it aloud once. Keep the passage open for reference. Who, in your group, manifests one of these qualities? Take these specific descriptions of love and apply them to your group. If, for example, Jim, John, Joan, Jean and Joe are your group, someone might call out, "Jean is not puffed up." "Joe is never rude." "John is not boastful."

Between each brief affirmation that, indeed, we love well, leave a quiet moment so that the affirmation might sink in. Conclude with a prayer of thanksgiving for the gift of loving well, your own gift and that of others. This activity will work well in a family too.

Your group might compose your own hymn of love, listing concrete and contemporary ways to love well. At a later meeting, if you can have the hymn duplicated, you might again apply certain lines to individual members.

By now your group should know each other quite well. This exercise asks you to celebrate the gifts of one another in the context of a prayer service.

Take a sheet of paper for each member of the group. In silence, look at someone and remember his or her gifts shared in this group, or gifts you've observed in other situations. List these gifts under the member's name.

Begin a new sheet for the second person, for the third, and so on. Collect all papers for John in one pile, Jean in another. Then give the list of John's gifts to Jean, Jean's gifts to Joe, and so on. Let each list of gifts be read slowly, reverently, so that Joe, for example, is really proclaiming Jean's gifts publicly. At the end of the proclamation, give the lists to the one whose gifts they are.

Read 1 Corinthians 11:17-22 aloud. Celebrate a community supper in your group, but not as the unkind Corinthians did. Arrange for a pot-luck or covered dish dinner to begin your final meeting. Provide bread and wine (or grape juice).

Open with the Our Father as a prayer of reconciliation. Then share the food, eat most of the bread, drink most of the wine, talking and laughing as you normally would. When the main dish is finished let one person take some bread and wine and raise it up, while another person reads 1 Corinthians 11:23-26.

Serve dessert. Then share how you felt about this community supper. Where was Jesus in it? How will he keep you "one" now that your meetings have ended? Ask him; then share your responses. At the end of the evening ask someone to bless the group, and close with a kiss of peace.

Conclusion

We conclude our journey through Scripture, but only with this book. God continues always and everywhere to come close. The Spirit continues to teach us. The risen Christ continues his mission and ministry in the world through us. He is our pioneer.

Pioneers cut through the underbrush, blaze the trail, forge into wilderness, break into newness. Jesus is our pioneer and he has done all that. With our eyes fixed on Jesus, we are urged to throw off every burden to which we cling and run the race after him (Hebrews 12:1-2).

Like Jesus before us, we are prophets chosen to speak God's word of comfort or challenge. We are to be God's disciples, listening and learning continually. We are missioned by God, sent surely to our families and communities, but sent also to whomever we find suffering or outcast. We are apostles if we have experienced that Jesus is risen, alive, life-giving. We are God's agents, ambassadors of reconciliation. Through us, God so loves the world, God comes close.

We have work to do. Yet, the work God wants is that we believe in Jesus (John 6:29). To believe is to be attached, to be united with. To believe is to embody Jesus. According to Pius XII, we the Church are Jesus Christ prolonged in space and time and communicated to humankind. We are the body of Christ, the risen Lord's only means of expressing himself in the world of today.

A biblical spirituality is a bodily spirituality. The body politic, the body-Church, and the human body provide the place for God's activity in history. The body, both the body of Jesus and our own bodies too, provides God with a way to come close, to express *hesed* and *'emet*. The Word took flesh and is alive living among us, in us and through us.

Hopefully we are more at home with the word of God expressed in the Scriptures, more at home with the Word made flesh, Jesus. If we make Christ's word our home, then we will be his disciples. We will know the truth and the truth will set us free (John 8:32). That is his promise and he is faithful. May he continue to bless us all with his *hesed*, his fidelity and his freedom.

About the Author

Rea McDonnell is a School Sister of Notre Dame from the Chicago province. Currently she serves as a pastoral counselor and spiritual director at the Consultation Center in Silver Spring, Maryland. She also is an adjunct associate professor in graduate training programs in ministry in Boston, in Philadelphia, and at the Washington Theological Union.

Rea has taught on every grade level (except first grade) through doctoral studies, and spent nine years as administrator of continuing education programs at the Washington Theological Union in Silver Spring. Her doctorate is a PhD in Biblical Studies from Boston University, and her own continuing education led her to certification by the Institute of Pastoral Psychotherapy, Oakton, Virginia, as well as membership in the American Association of Pastoral Counselors.

Author of some 60 articles on topics of prayer, ministry, scripture and spirituality, she has also authored four books on biblical spirituality, including *Catholic Epistles and Hebrews* (Michael Glazier, 1986). With Rachel Callahan, CSC, her psychologist colleague at the Consultation Center, she has co-authored, for Paulist Press: *Hope for Healing: Good News for Adult Children of Alcoholics* (1987); *Adult Children of Alcoholics: Ministers and the Ministries* (1990); and *Wholing the Heart: Good News for Those Who Grew Up in Troubled Families* (1991).

Rachel and Rea also team periodically, offering workshops along the East Coast.

St. Paul Book & Media Centers

ALASKA
750 West 5th Ave., Anchorage, AK 99501; 907-272-8183

CALIFORNIA
3908 Sepulveda Blvd., Culver City, CA 90230; 310-397-8676
5945 Balboa Ave., San Diego, CA 92111; 619-565-9181
46 Geary Street, San Francisco, CA 94108; 415-781-5180

FLORIDA
145 S.W. 107th Ave., Miami, FL 33174; 305-559-6715

HAWAII
1143 Bishop Street, Honolulu, HI 96813; 808-521-2731

ILLINOIS
172 North Michigan Ave., Chicago, IL 60601; 312-346-4228

LOUISIANA
4403 Veterans Memorial Blvd., Metairie, LA 70006; 504-887-7631

MASSACHUSETTS
50 St. Paul's Ave., Jamaica Plain, Boston, MA 02130; 617-522-8911
Rte. 1, 885 Providence Hwy., Dedham, MA 02026; 617-326-5385

MISSOURI
9804 Watson Rd., St. Louis, MO 63126; 314-965-3512

NEW JERSEY
561 U.S. Route 1, Wick Plaza, Edison, NJ 08817; 908-572-1200

NEW YORK
150 East 52nd Street, New York, NY 10022; 212-754-1110
78 Fort Place, Staten Island, NY 10301; 718-447-5071

OHIO
2105 Ontario Street, Cleveland, OH 44115; 216-621-9427

PENNSYLVANIA
214 W. DeKalb Pike, King of Prussia, PA 19406; 610-337-1882

SOUTH CAROLINA
243 King Street, Charleston, SC 29401; 803-577-0175

TENNESSEE
4811 Poplar Ave., Memphis, TN 38117; 901-761-0874

TEXAS
114 Main Plaza, San Antonio, TX 78205; 210-224-8101

VIRGINIA
1025 King Street, Alexandria, VA 22314; 703-549-3806

GUAM
285 Farenholt Avenue, Suite 308, Tamuning, Guam 96911; 671-646-7745

CANADA
3022 Dufferin Street, Toronto, Ontario, Canada M6B 3T5; 416-781-9131